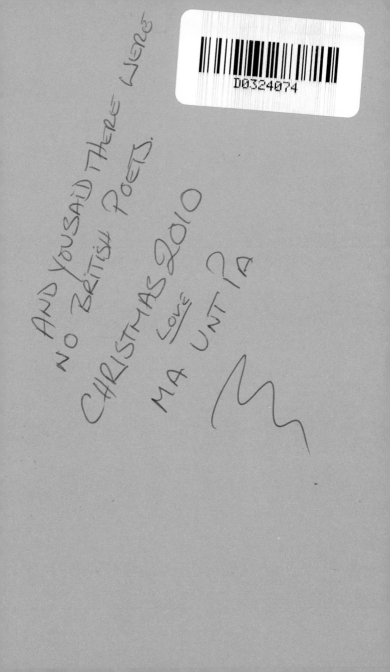

AND YOU SAID THERE WERE
NO BRITISH POETS.

CHRISTMAS 2010

LOVE

MA UNT PA

THE DOG IN BRITISH POETRY

THE DOG IN BRITISH POETRY

EDITED BY

R. MAYNARD LEONARD

CHRONICLE BOOKS
SAN FRANCISCO

TO THE CYNICS

PREFACE

While this collection of poems was being made, a well-known author and critic took occasion to gently ridicule anthologies and anthologists. He suggested, as if the force of foolishness could no further go, that the next anthology published would deal with dogs. Undismayed, however, by this, I persevered in my preparations, confident that the voice of the great dog-loving public in this country would drown that of the critic in question. It is rather remarkable that no one has yet published such a book as this. Nearly thirty years ago Mr. G. R. Jesse brought out very valuable 'Researches into the History of the British Dog,' but his two stout volumes chiefly consisted of prose. Miss Frances Power Cobbe has more recently written 'The Friend of Man—and his friends the Poets,' but she has contrived to cover after a fashion the literature of the whole civilised world in less than two hundred pages, and her chief object seems to have been to attack the practice of vivisection. The ground is, therefore, quite clear for the present volume, but I have to express my indebtedness to both Mr. Jesse and Miss Cobbe.

The poems that follow speak for themselves, and show sufficiently the place of the dog in British poetry. It

*would be superfluous to trace here the history of the dog
in this country, for that gigantic task has often been
attempted from the time of the 'learned Phisition and
good man,' Dr. Caius, to that of Mr. Hugh Dalziel in
recent years. I will only call attention to the fact that
the inhabitants of Great Britain have always highly
prized the dog, and we know, too, that the Romans set
great value on 'the painted Briton's pride.' If evidence
were needed with regard to the latter statement, I
have only to refer the reader to Whitaker's rendering of
Faliscus and Oppian, quoted in the Sporting Section. It
is interesting to observe in the following pages the light
in which successive generations have regarded the dog.
At first, for instance, we find that the poets seem to
consider a dog's prowess in the field to be its superlative
merit. It is the 'hound' that they celebrate, and they
seldom condescend to distinguish between the 'thousand
families' to which Tickell has referred. Perhaps,
incidentally, they admit the animal's usefulness as a
guardian of the sheepfold or of the dwelling-house, but
they are seldom so unstinting in their praise as
Camerarius as translated by Molle. Homer, it will be
remembered, makes Odysseus, wishing to hide his
feelings, ask depreciatingly whether old Argus has been
kept merely for ornament; and Homer is the father of
the poets as Plato is of the philosophers. Later we find
the hound giving place to the lap-dog, extolled in
characteristic fashion by Swift and Gay. More modern
poets, on the other hand, do fitting honour to the dog.
There is no great poet of latter days who has not loved*

the dumb companionship of 'the friend of man,' although all who have described the dog have not done him equal justice in their verse. Pope's 'poor Indian,' it will be seen, was a pioneer of the belief of modern poets in canine immortality.

I trust that my arrangement of the poems will commend itself. The notes are fuller than those generally supplied to collections of verse, but I have striven to make them more than ordinarily interesting. In the notes will be found my acknowledgments to those authors and publishers who have so kindly given me permission to quote copyright poems. Anonymous verse I have used as sparingly as possible, for the sentiment of the great unknown is more creditable than their style. On the other hand, I have admitted translations from dead languages, but only when done by standard poets. In view of the fact that this book is intended for the general reader, I have not hesitated to omit several passages from various poems, and have moreover modernised the spelling of the more ancient authors.

It was never my intention to gather together a complete collection of even British poems about dogs. I have sought to secure a representative rather than an exhaustive anthology, and I believe that I have overlooked no poem bearing directly on dogs that is of any great importance. It has not been possible, however, in every case to gain permission to reproduce copyright poems.

Scott has well said, 'The Almighty, who gave the dog to be the companion of our pleasures and our toils, hath invested him with a nature noble and incapable of deceit.'

The subject-matter of this volume needs no apology. 'An honest dog's a nobler theme by far,' as Bloomfield declares, than many a one chosen by the poets. I am not concerned to defend the merits of the following verse. Most of the poems are good, but some, certainly, do not reach a high poetic standard; yet I hope that all will be found interesting, even by the cynics to whom I have flung my glove. With regard to some, the reader may very properly bear in mind Cowper's request:

'Spare the poet for the subject's sake.'

ROBERT MAYNARD LEONARD.

CONTENTS

PART I.—*Narrative Poems*

CONTENTS

PART II.—*Sporting Poems*

CONTENTS

CONTENTS

PART IV.—*Miscellaneous Poems*

CONTENTS

CONTENTS

PART I

NARRATIVE POEMS

Of the dog in ancient story
Many a pleasant tale is told.

MARY HOWITT.

BRUCE AND THE BLOODHOUND

THE CHASE BY JOHN OF LORNE

John had eight hundred men and mo',
A sleuth-hound had he there also
Sae gude, that change wald for nae thing;
And some men say yet that the king
As a traitor him nursit had,
And ay sae mickle of him made,
That with his hand he wald him feed;
He followit him where'er he gaed,
Sae that the hound him lovit sae
That he wald part nae wise him frae.
But how that John of Lorne him had
I ne'er heard any mention made;
But men say it was certain thing
That he had him in his keeping,
And thro' him thocht to take the King.

Then John of Lorne came to the place
Wherefrae the King departit was,
And in his trace the hound he set.

The King toward the wood is gane,
Weary for sweat and will of wane,
Into the wood soon entered he,
And held down toward a valley
Where thro' the wood a water ran.
Thither in great haste went he than,
And began to rest him there,
And said he micht nae further stir,
His man said, 'Sir, that may nocht be.'

The King said, 'Since that thou wilt sae
Gae forth, and I shall with thee gae.
But I have heard ofttimes say
That who entering a water way
Wald wade a bow-draucht, he should ger
Both the sleuth-hound and the leader
Tyne the sleuth men put him tae,
Prove we if it will now do sae.
For were yon devilish hound away
I reck nocht of those left, perfay.'

As he desirit they have done,
And enterit in the water soon,
And held on entering it their way,
And soon to the land gaed they,
And held their way as they did ere.

But the sleuth-hound made stinting there,
And waverit long time to and frae
That he no certain gait could gae,
Till at the last then John of Lorne
Perceived the hound the sleuth had lorn,

And said, 'We have tynt this travail
To pass further may nocht avail.'

Barbour.

II

THE RAPE OF CHANTICLEER

THE silly widow and her daughters two,
Herden these hens' cry and maken woe,
And out at the doors starten they anon,
And saw the fox toward the wood is gone,
And bare upon his back the cock away:
They crieden out, 'Harow and wa la wa!
A ha the fox!' and after him they ran,
And eke with staves many another man;
Ran Colle our dog, and Talbot, and Gerland,
And Malkin with her distaff in her hand;
Ran cow and calf, and eke the very hogs,
So fearèd were for barking of the dogs.

Chaucer.

III

ON WALLACE'S TRACK

A HOUND that they had them among,
In Gyllisland there was that brachell bred,
Sicker of scent to follow them that fled.

Sae was she erst on Esk and on Ledaill;
When she got blude nae fleeing micht avail.
Then said they all, Wallace micht nocht away,
He should be theirs for ought that he do may.

The Englishmen has missit him; in hy
The hound they took, and followit hastily.
At the Gask wood full fain he wald have been,
But this sleuth brach whilk sicker was and
    keen
On Wallace foot followit sae felon fast
While in their sight they 'proachit at the last.
Their horse was wicht, had sojourned well and
    lang;
To the next wood twa mile they had to gang
Of upwith yird; they gaed with all their micht,
Gude hope they had, for it was near the nicht.
Fawdoun tirit, and said he micht nocht gang,
Wallace was wae to leave him in that thrang.
He bade him gae, and said the strength was
    near,
But he therefore wald nocht faster him stir.
Wallace in ire on the craig can him ta'
With his gude sword, and strak the head him
    frae,
Dreidless to ground derfly he dashit dead;
Frae him he leapt, and left him in that stead.
Some deemis it to ill, and other some to gude,
And I say here, into their termis rude,
Better it was he did, as thinkis me.
First, to the hound it micht great stoppin' be.

The power came, and suddenly him found:
For their sleuth-hound the straight gait to him
    gaed,
Of other trade she took as then nae heed
The sleuth stoppit, at Fawdoun still she stude,
Nor further she wald, frae time she found the
    blude.

Harry the Minstrel.

IV

THE BATTLE ABOUT A DOG

The Pictis houndis were nocht of sic speed
As Scottis houndis, nor yet sae gude at need,
Nor in sic game they were nocht half sae gude,
Nor of sic pleasure, nor sic pulchritude.
The King therefore he did give every man
Of the best houndis were among them than,
At their pleasure that time they were nocht
    spared
With horse and hound and all other reward.

This noble King, of whom before I told,
One hound he had both curious and bold,
Pleasant but peir, and full of pulchritude,
Supple and swift and in all game richt gude:
All other houndis he did exceed sae far
As into licht the moon does near ilk star.

The young Pictis to him they took gude keep,
Soon in the nicht when all men were asleep
They stole this hound and many other mo'
After they had taken their leave to go.
Soon in the morn when that this hound was
    missed
There was no wight where he was gone that wist ;
Except the man that had the hound in care
Followit richt fast, and after him he fare.

The young lordis some scorpit with great scorn,
Saying again, Suppose he had sworn,
That dog again as then he should nocht get ;
And he richt well thocht that he should them let.
Richt hastily laid handis on the hound
In leash and collar wherewith he was bound,
Truly, he said, they wald him nocht deny.
One hasty man that stood him near hand by
Drew out ane knife that was of metal gude
And stickit him that same time where he stude.
Ane man of his that time that stood near by
The coronach (raised) with ane loud shout and
    cry.

They gatherit fast when they heard the shout,
The country men that dwelt near hand about,
And when the people has heard tell 'em plain
The hound was stolen, the Kingis servant slain
That had the hound that time into his cuir,
They micht nocht thole no longer that injure.
All made ane vow revengit for to be
Of that great wrong, or all there for to dee.

And there was slain, if I richt understude,
Sixty Scottis that were men of gude ;
Ane hundred Pictis fighting on that plain,
Into that field that same day was slain.

Stewart.

V

ODYSSEUS AND THE SWINEHERD

MASTIFFS, as austere
As savage beasts, lay ever, their fierce strain
Bred by the herdsman, a mere prince of men,
Their number four. . . .
The fate-born-dogs-to-bark took sudden view
Of Odysseus, and upon him flew
With open mouth.   He, cunning to appal
A fierce dog's fury, from his hand let fall
His staff to earth, and sat him careless down.
And yet to him had one foul wrong been shown
Where most his right lay, had not instantly
The herdsman let his hide fall, and his cry
(With frequent stones flung at the dogs) repelled
This way and that their eager course they held ;
When through the entry port, he thus did mourn :
'O father ! how soon had you near been torn
By these rude dogs, whose hurt had branded me
With much neglect of you !'

Chapman.

VI

TREACHEROUS TOWSER

THERE dwelt a farmer in the west,
　　As we 're in story told ;
Whose herds were large and flocks the best
　　That ever lined a fold.

Armed with a staff, his russet coat,
　　And Towser by his side—
Early and late he tuned his throat
　　And every wolf defied.

Loved Towser was his heart's delight,
　　In cringe and fawning skilled,
Entrusted with the flocks by night,
　　And guardian of the field.

' Towser,' quoth he, ' I 'm for a fair ;
　　Be regent in my room :
Pray of my tender flocks take care,
　　And keep all safe at home.

' I know thee watchful, just, and brave,
　　Right worthy such a place ;
No wily fox shall thee deceive,
　　Nor wolf dare show his face.'

But ne'er did wolves a fold infest,
　　At regent Towser's rate :
He dined and supped upon the best,
　　And frequent breakfasts ate.

The farmer oft received advice,
     And laughed at the report ;
But, coming on him by surprise,
     Just found him at the sport.

' Ungrateful beast,' quoth he, ' what means
     That bloody mouth and paws ?
I know the base, the treacherous stains,
     Thy breach of trust and laws.

' The fruits of my past love I see ;
     Roger, the halter bring ;
E'en truss him on that pippin-tree,
     And let friend Towser swing.'

Yalden.

VII

THE YELPING NUISANCE OF THE WAY

A village cur, of snappish race,
The pertest puppy of the place,
Imagined that his treble throat
Was blest with music's sweetest note ;
In the mid road he basking lay,
The yelping nuisance of the way ;
For not a creature passed along,
But had a sample of his song.
Soon as the trotting steed he hears,
He starts, he cocks his dapper ears ;

Away he scours, assaults his hoof,
Now near him snarls, now barks aloof;
With shrill impertinence attends,
Nor leaves him till the village ends.
It chanced upon his evil day,
A Pad came pacing down the way;
The cur with never-ceasing tongue,
Upon the passing traveller sprung.
The horse, provoked from scorn to ire,
Flung backwards: rolling in the mire,
The puppy howled, and bleeding lay;
The Pad in peace pursued his way.

A shepherd's dog, who saw the deed,
Detesting the vexatious breed,
Bespoke him thus: ' When coxcombs prate,
They kindle wrath, contempt, or hate:
Thy teasing tongue had judgment tied,
Thou hadst not like a puppy died.'

Gay.

VIII

THE MEDDLING MASTIFF

*Those who in quarrels interpose
Must often wipe a bloody nose.*

A MASTIFF, of true English blood,
Loved fighting better than his food.
When dogs were snarling for a bone,
He longed to make the war his own,
And often found (when two contend)
To interpose obtained his end.

He gloried in his limping pace;
The scars of honour seamed his face;
In ev'ry limb a gash appears,
And frequent fights retrenched his ears.
   As on a time he heard from far
Two dogs engaged in noisy war,
Away he scours and lays about him,
Resolved no fray should be without him.
Forth from his yard a tanner flies,
And to the bold intruder cries:
   'A cudgel shall correct your manners:
Whence sprang this cursèd hate of tanners?
While on my dog you vent your spite,
Sirrah! 'tis me you dare not bite.'
To see the battle thus perplexed,
With equal rage a butcher, vexed,
Hoarse-screaming from the circled crowd
To the cursed mastiff cries aloud:
   'Both Hockleyhole and Mary'bone
The combats of my dog have known:
He ne'er, like bullies coward-hearted,
Attacks in public to be parted.
Think not, rash fool, to share his fame;
Be his the honour—or the shame.'
   Thus said, they swore, and raved like
     thunder,
Then dragged their fastened dogs asunder;
While clubs and kicks from every side
Rebounded from the mastiff's hide.
All reeking now with sweat and blood,
Awhile the parted warriors stood;

Then poured upon the meddling foe,
Who, worried, howled and sprawled below.
He rose ; and limping from the fray,
By both sides mangled, sneaked away.

Gay.

IX

THE TURNSPIT TAUGHT

' THE dinner must be dished at one ;
Where 's this vexatious turnspit gone ?
Unless the skulking cur is caught,
The sirloin 's spoilt, and I 'm in fault.'
Thus said (for sure you 'll think it fit
That I the cook-maid's oaths omit),
With all the fury of a cook,
Her cooler kitchen Nan forsook :
The broom-stick o'er her head she waves,
She sweats, she stamps, she puffs, she raves—
The sneaking cur before her flies ;
She whistles, calls, fair speech she tries ;
These nought avail.   Her choler burns ;
The fist and cudgel threat by turns.
With hasty stride she presses near ;
He slinks aloof, and howls with fear.

' Was ever cur so cursed (he cried) !
What star did at my birth preside !
Am I for life by compact bound
To tread the wheel's eternal round ?

Inglorious task ! of all our race
No slave is half so mean and base.
Had fate a kinder lot assigned,
And formed me of the lap-dog kind,
I then, in higher life employed,
Had indolence and ease enjoyed ;
And, like a gentleman, caressed,
Had been the lady's favourite guest ;
Or were I sprung from spaniel line,
Was his sagacious nostril mine,
By me, their never-erring guide,
From wood and plain their feasts supplied,
Knights, squires, attendant on my pace,
Had shared the pleasures of the chase.'

An ox by chance o'erheard his moan,
And thus rebuked the lazy drone :
'You by the duties of your post
Shall turn the spit when I 'm the roast ;
And for reward shall share the feast—
I mean shall pick my bones, at least.'
   'Till now (th' astonished cur replies)
I looked on all with envious eyes. . . .
Let envy then no more torment :
Think on the ox, and learn content.'
Thus said, close following at her heel,
With cheerful heart he mounts the wheel.

Gay.

x

ARGUS

WHEN wise Ulysses, from his native coast
Long kept by wars, and long by tempests tost,
Arrived at last—poor, old, disguised, alone,
To all his friends and ev'n his queen unknown,
Changed as he was, with age, and toils, and
    cares,
Furrowed his rev'rend face, and white his hairs,
In his own palace forced to ask his bread,
Scorned by those slaves his former bounty fed,
Forgot of all his own domestic crew,
His faithful dog his rightful master knew!
Unfed, unhoused, neglected, on the clay,
Like an old servant, now cashiered, he lay;
And though ev'n then expiring on the plain,
Touched with resentment of ungrateful man,
And longing to behold his ancient lord again.
Him when he saw, he rose, and crawled to meet,
('Twas all he could), and fawned, and kissed his
    feet,
Seized with dumb joy; then falling by his side,
Owned his returning lord, looked up, and died.

Pope.

XI

THE MAD DOG

Good people all, of every sort,
　　Give ear unto my song,
And if you find it wondrous short—
　　It cannot hold you long.

In Islington there was a man,
　　Of whom the world might say :
That still a godly race he ran—
　　Whene'er he went to pray.

A kind and gentle heart he had,
　　To comfort friends and foes ;
The naked every day he clad—
　　When he put on his clothes.

And in that town a dog was found,
　　As many dogs there be,
Both mongrel, puppy, whelp and hound,
　　And curs of low degree.

This dog and man at first were friends ;
　　But when a pique began,
The dog, to gain some private ends,
　　Went mad, and bit the man.

Around from all the neighbouring streets
　　The wondering neighbours ran,
And swore the dog had lost his wits,
　　To bite so good a man.

The wound it seemed both sore and sad
    To every Christian eye ;
And while they swore the dog was mad,
    They swore the man would die.

But soon a wonder came to light,
    That showed the rogues they lied :
The man recovered of the bite—
    The dog it was that died.

Goldsmith.

XII

BEAU AND THE WATER LILY

THE noon was shady, and soft airs
    Swept Ouse's silent tide,
When 'scaped from literary cares,
    I wandered on his side.

My spaniel, prettiest of his race,
    And high in pedigree
(Two nymphs adorned with every grace.
    That spaniel found for me),

Now wantoned lost in flags and reeds,
    Now starting into sight,
Pursued the swallow o'er the meads,
    With scarce a slower flight.

It was the time that Ouse displayed
 His lilies newly blown ;
Their beauties I intent surveyed,
 And one I wished my own.

With cane extended far I sought
 To steer it close to land ;
But still the prize, though nearly caught,
 Escaped my eager hand.

Beau marked my unsuccessful pains
 With fixed considerate face,
And puzzling set his puppy brains
 To comprehend the case.

But with a chirrup clear and strong,
 Dispersing all his dream,
I thence withdrew, and followed long
 The windings of the stream.

My ramble ended, I returned ;
 Beau, trotting far before,
The floating wreath again discerned,
 And, plunging, left the shore.

I saw him, with that lily cropped,
 Impatient swim to meet
My quick approach, and soon he dropped
 The treasure at my feet.

Charmed with the sight, 'The world,' I cried,
 'Shall hear of this thy deed :
My dog shall mortify the pride
 Of man's superior breed :

But chief myself I will enjoin,
　　Awake at duty's call,
To show a love as prompt as thine,
　　To Him who gives me all.'

Cowper.

XIII

INFALLIBLE DOUSSIEKIE

THERE was a wee bit wifukie was comin' frae
　　the fair,
Had got a wee bit drappukie, that bred her
　　meikle care,
It gaed about the wifie's heart, and she began
　　to spew :
Oh! quo' the wee wifukie, I wish I binna fou.
I wish I binna fou, quo' she, I wish I binna fou,
Oh! quo' the wee wifukie, I wish I binna fou.

If Johnnie find me barley-sick, I'm sure he'll
　　claw my skin ;
But I'll lie down and tak' a nap before that I
　　gae in.
Sitting at the dyke-side, and taking o' her nap,
By came a packman laddie wi' a little pack,
Wi' a little pack, *etc.*

He's clippit a' her gowden locks, sae bonnie
　　and sae lang,
He's ta'en her purse and a' her placks, and fast
　　awa he ran ;

And when the wifie wakened, her head was like
 a bee :
Oh ! quo' the wee wifukie, this is nae me.
This is nae me, quo' she, this is nae me,
Somebody has been felling me, and this is nae
 me.

I have a little housikie, but and a kindly man ;
A dog, they ca' him Doussiekie, if this be me
 he 'll fawn.

The night was late, and dang out weet, and oh !
 but it was dark,
The doggie heard a body's foot, and he began
 to bark ;
Oh ! when she heard the doggie bark, and
 kennin' it was he,
Oh ! weel ken ye, Doussie, quo' she, this is nae
 me,
This is nae me, *etc.*

       Geddes.

XIV

THE MISER'S ONLY FRIEND

THERE watched a cur before the miser's gate—
A very cur, whom all men seemed to hate ;
Gaunt, savage, shaggy, with an eye that shone
Like a live coal, and he possessed but one :

His bark was wild and eager, and became
That meagre body and that eye of flame;
His master prized him much, and Fang his name.
His master fed him largely; but not that,
Nor aught of kindness, made the snarler fat;
Flesh he devoured, but not a bit would stay—
He barked, and snarled, and growled it all away.
His ribs were seen extended like a rack,
And coarse red hair hung roughly o'er his back.
Lamed in one leg, and bruised in wars of yore,
Now his sore body made his temper sore.
Such was the friend of him who could not find,
Nor make him, one 'mong creatures of his kind.
Brave deeds of Fang his master often told,
The son of Fury, famed in deeds of old,
From Snatch and Rabid sprung; and noted they
In earlier times—each dog will have his day.

The notes of Fang were to his master known,
And dear—they bore some likeness to his own;
For both conveyed to the experienced ear,
' I snarl and bite because I hate and fear.'
None passed ungreeted by the master's door,
Fang railed at all, but chiefly at the poor;
And when the nights were stormy, cold, and
      dark,
The act of Fang was a perpetual bark;
But though the master loved the growl of Fang,
There were who vowed the ugly cur to hang;
Whose angry master, watchful for his friend,
As strongly vowed his servant to defend.

In one dark night, and such as Fang before
Was ever known its tempests to outroar,
To his protector's wonder now expressed,
No angry notes—his anger was at rest.
The wond'ring master sought the silent yard,
Left Phœbe sleeping, and his door unbarred ;
Nor more returned to that forsaken bed—
But lo ! the morning came, and he was dead.
Fang and his master side by side were laid
In grim repose—their debt of nature paid.
The master's hand upon the cur's cold chest
Was now reclined, and had before been pressed,
As if he searched how deep and wide the wound
That laid such spirit in a sleep so sound ;
And when he found it was the sleep of death,
A sympathising sorrow stopped his breath.
Close to his trusty servant he was found,
As cold his body, and his sleep as sound.

Crabbe.

XV

THE TWA DOGS

'Twas in that place o' Scotland's isle,
That bears the name o' Auld King Coil,
Upon a bonie day in June,
When wearing thro' the afternoon,
Twa dogs, that werena thrang at hame,
Forgather'd ance upon a time.

The first I'll name, they ca'd him Cæsar
Was keepit for his Honour's pleasure :
His hair, his size, his mouth, his lugs,
Show'd he was nane o' Scotland's dogs ;
But whalpit some place far abroad,
Whare sailors gang to fish for cod.

His lockèd, letter'd, braw brass collar,
Show'd him the gentleman and scholar ;
But tho' he was o' high degree,
The fient a pride—nae pride had he ;
But wad hae spent an hour caressin',
Ev'n wi' a tinkler-gipsey's messin.
At kirk or market, mill or smiddie,
Nae tawted tyke, tho' e'er sae duddie,
But he wad stan't, as glad to see him,
An' stroan't on stanes and hillocks wi' him.

The tither was a ploughman's collie,
A rhyming, ranting, raving billie,
Wha for his friend and comrade had him,
An' in his freaks had Luath ca'd him,
After some dog in Highland sang,
Was made lang syne,—Lord knows how
        lang.

He was a gash an' faithfu' tyke,
As ever lap a sheugh or dyke.
His honest, sonsie, baws'nt face,
Ay gat him friends in ilka place ;
His breast was white, his touzie back
Weel clad wi' coat o' glossy black ;
His gawcie tail, wi' upward curl,
Hung o'er his hurdies wi' a swirl.

Nae doubt but they were fain o' ither,
An' unco pack an' thick thegither;
Wi' social nose whyles snuff'd and snowkit;
Whyles mice and moudiewarts they howkit;
Whyles scour'd awa in lang excursion,
An' worry'd ither in diversion;
Until wi' daffin weary grown,
Upon a knowe they sat them down,
And there began a lang digression
About the lords o' the creation.

  *   *   *   *

   The sun was out o' sight,
An' darker gloamin' brought the night;
The bum-clock humm'd wi' lazy drone,
The kye stood rowtin' i' the loan;
When up they gat, an' shook their lugs,
Rejoiced they werena *men* but *dogs*;
An' each took aff his several way,
Resolved to meet some ither day.

          Burns.

XVI

BARRY, THE ST. BERNARD

      When the storm
Rose, and the snow rolled on in ocean-waves,
When on his face the experienced traveller fell,
Sheltering his lips and nostrils with his hands,
Then all was changed; and, sallying with their
  pack

Into that blank of nature, they became
Unearthly beings. 'Anselm, higher up,
Just where it drifts, a dog howls loud and long,
And now, as guided by a voice from Heaven,
Digs with his feet. That noble vehemence,
Whose can it be, but his who never erred?
A man lies underneath! Let us to work.'

Rogers.

XVII

BETH GELERT

THE spearman heard the bugle sound,
　　And cheerly smiled the morn;
And many a brach, and many a hound,
　　Obeyed Llewellyn's horn.

And still he blew a louder blast,
　　And gave a louder cheer:
'Come, Gelert, come, wert never last
　　Llewellyn's horn to hear!

Oh, where does faithful Gelert roam?
　　The flower of all his race!
So true, so brave—a lamb at home,
　　A lion in the chase!'

'Twas only at Llewellyn's board
　　The faithful Gelert fed;
He watched, he served, he cheered his lord,
　　And sentineled his bed.

In sooth, he was a peerless hound,
  The gift of Royal John ;
But now no Gelert could be found,
  And all the chase rode on.

And now, as o'er the rocks and dells,
  The gallant chidings rise,
All Snowdon's craggy chaos yells
  With many-mingled cries.

That day Llewellyn little loved
  The chase of hart or hare ;
And scant and small the booty proved,
  For Gelert was not there.

Unpleased Llewellyn homeward hied,
  When, near the portal-seat,
His truant, Gelert, he espied,
  Bounding his lord to greet.

But when he gained his castle-door,
  Aghast the chieftain stood ;
The hound all o'er was smeared with gore—
  His lips, his fangs ran blood !

Llewellyn gazed with fierce surprise,
  Unused such looks to meet,
His favourite checked his joyful guise,
  And crouched and licked his feet.

Onward in haste Llewellyn passed—
  And on went Gelert too—
And still, where'er his eyes were cast,
  Fresh blood-gouts shocked his view !

O'erturned his infant's bed he found,
　The bloodstained covert rent;
And all around, the walls and ground,
　With recent blood besprent.

He called his child—no voice replied;
　He searched—with terror wild.
Blood! blood! he found on every side,
　But nowhere found the child!

'Hell-hound! my child's by thee devoured!'
　The frantic father cried;
And, to the hilt, his vengeful sword
　He plunged in Gelert's side!

His suppliant looks, as prone he fell,
　No pity could impart;
But still his Gelert's dying yell
　Passed heavy o'er his heart.

Aroused by Gelert's dying yell,
　Some slumberer wakened nigh:
What words the parent's joy can tell,
　To hear his infant cry?

Concealed beneath a tumbled heap,
　His hurried search had missed,
All glowing from his rosy sleep,
　The cherub-boy he kissed.

Nor scathe had he, nor harm, nor dread—
　But the same couch beneath
Lay a gaunt wolf, all torn and dead—
　Tremendous still in death!

Ah, what was then Llewellyn's pain,
　For now the truth was clear:
The gallant hound the wolf had slain,
　To save Llewellyn's heir.

Vain, vain was all Llewellyn's woe ;
　'Best of thy kind, adieu !
The frantic deed which laid thee low
　This heart shall ever rue !'

And now a gallant tomb they raise,
　With costly sculpture decked;
And marbles, storied with his praise,
　Poor Gelert's bones protect.

Here never could the spearman pass,
　Or forester, unmoved ;
Here oft the tear-besprinkled grass
　Llewellyn's sorrow proved.

And here he hung his horn and spear ;
　And there, as evening fell,
In fancy's ear he oft would hear
　Poor Gelert's dying yell.

And, till great Snowdon's rocks grow old,
　And cease the storm to brave.
The consecrated spot shall hold
　The name of ' Gelert's Grave.'

　　　　　　　　　　　　Spencer.

XVIII

A DOG'S TRAGEDY

On his morning rounds the Master
Goes to learn how all things fare ;
Searches pasture after pasture,
Sheep and cattle eyes with care ;
And, for silence or for talk,
He hath comrades in his walk ;
Four dogs, each pair of different breed,
Distinguished two for scent, and two for speed.

See a hare before him started !
—Off they fly in earnest chase ;
Every dog is eager-hearted,
All the four are in the race :
And the hare whom they pursue
Knows from instinct what to do ;
Her hope is near : no turn she makes ;
But, like an arrow, to the river takes.

Deep the river was, and crusted
Thinly by a one night's frost ;
But the nimble hare hath trusted
To the ice, and safely crost ;
She hath crost, and without heed
All are following at full speed,
When, lo ! the ice, so thinly spread,
Breaks—and the greyhound, Dart, is over head !

Better fate have Prince and Swallow—
See them cleaving to the sport!
Music has no heart to follow,
Little Music, she stops short.
She hath neither wish nor heart,
Hers is now another part:
A loving creature she, and brave!
And fondly strives her struggling friend to save.

From the brink her paws she stretches,
Very hands as you would say!
And afflicting moans she fetches,
As he breaks the ice away.
For herself she hath no fears,—
Him alone she sees and hears,—
Makes efforts with complainings; nor gives o'er
Until her fellow sinks to re-appear no more.

Wordsworth.

XIX

FIDELITY

A BARKING sound the Shepherd hears,
A cry as of a dog or fox;
He halts—and searches with his eyes
Among the scattered rocks:
And now at distance can discern
A stirring in a brake of fern;
And instantly a dog is seen,
Glancing through that covert green.

The Dog is not of mountain breed ;
Its motions, too, are wild and shy ;
With something, as the Shepherd thinks,
Unusual in its cry :
Nor is there any one in sight
All round, in hollow or on height ;
Nor shout, nor whistle strikes his ear ;
What is the creature doing here ?

It was a cove, a huge recess,
That keeps, till June, December's snow ;
A lofty precipice in front,
A silent tarn below !
Far in the bosom of Helvellyn,
Remote from public road or dwelling,
Pathway, or cultivated land,
From trace of human foot or hand.

There sometimes doth a leaping fish
Send through the tarn a lonely cheer ;
The crags repeat the raven's croak,
In symphony austere ;
Thither the rainbow comes—the cloud—
And mists that spread the flying shroud ;
And sunbeams ; and the sounding blast,
That, if it could, would hurry past ;
But that enormous barrier holds it fast.

Not free from boding thoughts, a while
The Shepherd stood ; then makes his way
O'er rocks and stones, following the Dog
As quickly as he may ;

Nor far had gone before he found
A human skeleton on the ground;
The appalled Discoverer with a sigh
Looks round, to learn the history.

From those abrupt and perilous rocks
The Man had fallen, that place of fear!
At length upon the Shepherd's mind
It breaks, and all is clear:
He instantly recalled the name,
And who he was, and whence he came;
Remembered, too, the very day
On which the Traveller passed this way.

But hear a wonder, for whose sake
This lamentable tale I tell!
A lasting monument of words
This wonder merits well.
The Dog, which still was hovering nigh,
Repeating the same timid cry,
This Dog had been through three months' space
A dweller in that savage place.

Yes, proof was plain that, since the day
When this ill-fated Traveller died,
The Dog had watched about the spot,
Or by his master's side:
How nourished here through such long time
He knows, who gave that love sublime;
And gave that strength of feeling, great
Above all human estimate!

                                    Wordsworth.

XX

THE WANDERER'S DOG

I CLIMBED the dark brow of the mighty Helvellyn,
    Lakes and mountains beneath me gleamed
      misty and wide ;
All was still, save by fits, when the eagle was
    yelling,
    And starting around me the echoes replied.
On the right, Striden Edge round the Red Tarn
    was bending,
And Catchedicam its left verge was defending,
One huge nameless rock in the front was
    ascending,
    When I marked the sad spot where the
      wanderer had died.

Dark green was that spot 'mid the brown
    mountain-heather,
    Where the Pilgrim of Nature lay stretched
      in decay,
Like the corpse of an outcast abandoned to
    weather,
    Till the mountain winds wasted the tenant-
      less clay.
Nor yet quite deserted, though lonely extended,
For, faithful in death, his mute favourite attended,
The much-loved remains of her master defended,
    And chased the hill-fox and the raven away.

How long didst thou think that his silence was
      slumber ?
  When the wind waved his garment, how oft
      didst thou start ?
How many long days and long weeks didst thou
      number,
  Ere he faded before thee, the friend of thy
      heart ?
And, oh ! was it meet, that—no requiem read
      o'er him—
No mother to weep, and no friend to deplore
      him,
And thou, little guardian, alone stretched before
      him—
  Unhonoured the Pilgrim from life should
      depart !

When a Prince to the fate of the Peasant has
      yielded,
  The tapestry waves dark round the dim-
      lighted hall ;
With scutcheons of silver the coffin is shielded,
  And pages stand mute by the canopied pall :
Through the courts, at deep midnight, the torches
      are gleaming ;
In the proudly-arched chapel the banners are
      beaming,
Far adown the long aisle sacred music is stream-
      ing,
  Lamenting a Chief of the people should fall.

But meeter for thee, gentle lover of nature,
    To lay down thy head like the meek moun-
      tain lamb,
When, 'wildered, he drops from some cliff huge
    in stature,
    And draws his last sob by the side of his
      dam.
And more stately thy couch by this desert lake
    lying,
Thy obsequies sung by the grey plover flying,
With one faithful friend but to witness thy
    dying,
    In the arms of Helvellyn and Catchedicam.

Scott.

XXI

BRANKSOME'S HEIR AND THE HOUND

For aye the more he sought his way
The farther still he went astray,
Until he heard the mountains round
Ring to the baying of a hound.

And hark ! and hark ! the deep-mouthed bark
    Comes nigher still, and nigher :
Bursts on the path a dark bloodhound,
His tawny muzzle tracked the ground,
    And his red eye shot fire.
Soon as the wildered child saw he
He flew at him right furiouslie.

I ween you would have seen with joy
The bearing of the gallant boy,
When, worthy of his noble sire,
His wet cheek glowed 'twixt fear and ire!
He faced the bloodhound manfully,
And held his little bat on high;
So fierce he struck, the dog, afraid,
At cautious distance hoarsely bayed.

Scott.

XXII

POOR YARROW

WHEN red hath set the beamless sun,
Through heavy vapours dark and dun;
When the tired ploughman, dry and warm,
Hears, half asleep, the rising storm
Hurling the hail and sleeted rain
Against the casement's tinkling pane;
The sounds that drive wild deer and fox
To shelter in the brake and rocks
Are warnings which the shepherd ask
To dismal and to dangerous task.
Oft he looks forth, and hopes, in vain,
The blast may sink in mellowing rain;
Till, dark above, and white below
Decided drives the flaky snow,
And forth the hardy swain must go.

Long, with dejected look and whine,
To leave the hearth the dogs repine ;
Whistling and cheering them to aid,
Around his back he wreathes his plaid :
His flock he gathers, and he guides
To open downs, and mountain-sides,
Where fiercest though the tempest blow
Least deeply lies the drift below.
The blast that whistles o'er the fells
Stiffens his locks to icicles ;
Oft he looks back, while streaming far
His cottage window seems a star,—
Loses its feeble gleam,—and then
Turns patient to the blast again,
And, facing to the tempest's sweep,
Drives through the gloom his lagging sheep.
If fails his heart, if his limbs fail,
Benumbing death is in the gale :
His paths, his landmarks, all unknown,
Close to the hut, no more his own,
Close to the aid he sought in vain,
The morn may find the stiffened swain :
His widow sees, at dawning pale,
His orphans raise their feeble wail ;
And, close beside him, in the snow,
Poor Yarrow, partner of their woe,
Couches upon his master's breast,
And licks his cheek to break his rest.

Scott.

XXIII

RODERICK'S FAITHFUL THERON

WHILE thus Florinda spake, the dog who lay
Before Rusilla's feet, eyeing him long
And wistfully, had recognised at length,
Changed as he was and in those sordid weeds,
His Royal master, and he rose and licked
His withered hand, and earnestly looked up
With eyes whose human meaning did not need
The aid of speech ; and moaned, as if at once
To court and chide the long-withheld caress.
A feeling uncommixed with sense of guilt
Or shame, yet painfullest, thrilled through the
    King ;
But he, to self-control now long inured,
Represt his rising heart, nor other tears,
Full as his struggling bosom was, let fall
Than seemed to follow on Florinda's words.
Looking toward them, yet so that still
He shunned the meeting of her eye, he said,
' Virtuous and pious as thou art, and ripe
For Heaven, O lady, I will think the man
Hath not by his good Angel been cast off
For whom thy supplications rise.'

              Thus having said,
Deliberately, in self-possession still,
Himself from that most painful interview
Dispeeding, he withdrew.   The watchful dog

Followed his footsteps close.   But he retired
Into the thickest grove; there yielding way
To his o'erburthened nature, from all eyes
Apart, he cast himself upon the ground,
And threw his arms around the dog, and cried,
While tears streamed down, 'Thou, Theron, thou
     hast known
Thy poor lost master . . . Theron, none but thou!'

Resting his head upon his master's knees
Upon the bank beside him Theron lay.
What matters change of state and circumstance
To him?   What matters it that Roderick wears
The crown no longer, nor the sceptre wields?
It is the dear-loved hand, whose friendly touch
Had flattered him so oft; it is the voice
At whose glad summons to the field so oft
From slumber he had started, shaking off
Dreams of the chase to share the actual joy;
The eye, whose recognition he was wont
To watch and welcome with exultant tongue.

A coming step, unheard by Roderick, roused
His watchful ear, and turning he beheld
Siverian.   'Father,' said the good old man,
'Hast thou some charm, which draws about thee
     thus
The hearts of all our house—even to the beast
That lacks discourse of reason, but too oft,
With uncorrupted feeling and dumb faith
Puts lordly man to shame?'

                         Robert Southey.

XXIV

A TALE OF THE REIGN OF TERROR

'Twas in a neighbouring land what time
　The Reign of Terror triumphed there,
And every horrid shape of crime
　Stalked out from murder's bloody lair.

'Twas in those dreadful times there dwelt
　In Lyons, the defiled with blood,
A loyal family, that felt
　The earliest fury of the flood.

Wife, children, friends, it swept away
　From wretched Valrive, one by one :
Himself severely doomed to stay
　Till everything he loved was gone—

A man proscribed, whom not to shun
　Was danger, almost fate, to brave.
So all forsook him, all save one—
　One humble, faithful, powerless slave :

His dog, old Nina.　She had been,
　When they were boys, his children's mate,
His gallant Claude, his mild Eugene,
　Both gone before him to their fate.

　　　*　　　*　　　*　　　*

They spurned her off—but ever more
  Surmounting e'en her timid nature,
Love brought her to the prison door,
    And there she crouched, fond faithful crea-
        ture!

Watching so long, so piteously,
  That e'en the jailer—man of guilt,
Of rugged heart—was moved to cry,
    'Poor wretch, there enter if thou wilt.'

And who than Nina more content,
  When she had gained that dreary cell,
Where lay in helpless dreariment
    The master loved so long and well?

And when into his arms she leapt,
  In her old fond familiar way,
And close into his bosom crept,
    And licked his face—a feeble ray

Of something—not yet comfort—stole
  Upon his heart's stern misery;
And his lips moved, 'Poor loving fool!
    Then *all* have not abandoned me.'

The hour by grudging kindness spared
  Expired too soon—the friends must part—
And Nina from the prison gazed,
    With lingering pace and heavy heart.

Shelter, and rest, and food she found
  With one who, for the master's sake,
Though grim suspicion stalked around,
  Dared his old servant home to take.

Beneath that friendly roof, each night
  She stayed, but still returning day—
Ay, the first beam of dawning light—
  Beheld her on her anxious way

Towards the prison, there to await
  The hour, when through that dismal door
The keeper, half compassionate,
  Should bid her enter as before.

And well she seemed to comprehend
  The time appointed for her stay,
The little hour that with her friend
  She tarried there, was all her day.

       *   *   *   *

At last the captive's summons came:
  They led him forth his doom to hear;
No tremor shook his thrice-nerved frame,
  Whose heart was dead to hope and fear.

So with calm step he moved along,
  And calmly faced the murderous crew,
But close and closer for the throng,
  Poor Nina to her master drew.

And she has found a resting-place
   Between his knees—her old safe home—
And she looks round in every face,
   As if to read his written doom.

'Twas but a step in those dread days
   From trial to the guillotine;
A moment: and Valrive surveys
   With steadfast eye the fell machine.

He mounts the platform—takes his stand
   Before the fatal block, and kneels
In preparation—but his hand
   A soft warm touch that moment feels.

His eyes glance downward, and a tear—
   The last tear they shall ever shed—
Falls, as he utters, 'Thou still here!'
   Upon his faithful servant's head.

Yes, she is there; that hellish shout,
   That deadly stroke, she hears them plain,
And from the headless trunk starts out
   Even over her the bloody rain.

      *   *   *   *

Old faithful Nina!   There lies she,
   Her cold head on the cold earth pressed,
As it was wont so lovingly
   To lie upon her master's breast.

And there she stayed the livelong day,
   Mute, motionless, her sad watch keeping,
A stranger who had passed that way
   Would have believed her dead or sleeping.

But if a step approached the grave,
   Her eye looked up with jealous care,
Imploringly, as if to crave
   That no rude foot should trample there.

That night she came not as of late
   To her old charitable home ;
The next day's sun arose and set,
   Night fell—and still she failed to come.

Then the third day her pitying host
   Went kindly forth to seek his guest,
And found her at her mournful post,
   Stretched quietly as if at rest.

Yet she was not asleep nor dead ;
   And when her master's friend she saw,
The poor old creature raised her head,
   And moaned, and moved one feeble paw ;

But stirred not thence—and all in vain
   He called, caressed her, would have led—
Tried threats—then coaxing words again—
   Brought food—she turned away her head.

So with kind violence at last
   He bore her home with gentle care ;
In her old shelter tied her fast,
   Placed food beside and left her there.

But ere the hour of rest, again
   He visited the captive's shed,
And there the cord lay, gnawed in twain—
   The food untasted—she was fled.

And, vexed, he cried, ' Perverse old creature !
   Well, let her go, I've done my best.'
But there was something in his nature,
   A feeling would not let him rest.

So with the early light once more
   Towards the burial-ground went he ;
And there he found her as before,
   But not as then stretched quietly ;

For she had worked the long night through,
   In the strong impulse of despair,
Down, down into the grave—and now,
   Panting and weak, still laboured there.

But death's cold stiffening frost benumbs
   Her limbs, and clouds her heavy eye—
And hark ! her feeble moan becomes
   A shriek of human agony ;

As if before her task was over
   She feared to die in her despair—
But see ! those last faint strokes uncover
   A straggling lock of thin grey hair.

One struggle, one convulsive start,
   And there the face beloved lies—
Now be at peace, thou faithful heart !—
   She licks the livid lips, and dies.

                  Caroline Bowles Southey.

XXV

THE DOG OF ST. BERNARD'S

They tell that on St. Bernard's mount,
   Where holy monks abide,
Still mindful of misfortune's claim,
   Though dead to all beside ;

The weary, way-worn traveller
   Oft sinks beneath the snow ;
For, were his faltering steps to bend,
   No track is left to show.

'Twas here, bewildered and alone,
   A stranger roamed at night ;
His heart was heavy as his tread,
   His scrip alone was light.

Onward he pressed, yet many an hour
   He had not tasted food ;
For many an hour he had not known
   Which way his footsteps trod ;

And if the Convent's bell had rung
   To hail the pilgrims near,
It still had rung in vain for him—
   He was too far to hear.

And should the morning light disclose
   Its towers amid the snow,
To him 'twould be a mournful sight—
   He had not strength to go.

Valour could arm no mortal man
   That night to meet the storm ;
No glow of pity could have kept
   A human bosom warm.

But obedience to a master's will
   Had taught the dog to roam,
And through the terrors of the waste
   To fetch the wanderer home.

He never loiters by the way,
   Nor lays him down to rest,
Nor seeks a refuge from the storm
   That pelts his generous breast.

And surely 'tis not less than joy
   That makes it throb so fast,
When he sees, extended on the snow,
   The wanderer found at last.

Eager emotion swelled his breast
   To tell the generous tale,
And he raised his voice to the loudest tone
   To bid the wanderer hail !

The pilgrim heard, he raised his head,
   And beheld the shaggy form,
With sudden fear he seized the gun
   That rested on his arm.

Fear gave him back his wasted strength,
   He took his aim too well,
The bullet bore the message home—
   The injured mastiff fell !

His eye was dimmed, his voice was still,
　　And he tossed his head no more ;
But his heart, though it ceased to throb with joy,
　　Was generous as before.

For round his willing neck he bore
　　A store of needful food,
That might support the traveller's strength
　　On the yet remaining road.

So he heeded not his aching wound,
　　But crawled to the traveller's side,
Marked with a look the way he came,
　　Then shuddered, groaned, and died.

　　　　　　　　　Caroline Fry (Wilson).

XXVI

SANCHO, THE BAGMAN'S DOG

Stant littore Puppies.—Virgil.

It was a litter, a litter of five,
Four are drowned, and one left alive,
He was thought worthy alone to survive ;
And the Bagman resolved upon bringing him up,
To eat of his bread and drink of his cup,
He was such a dear little cock-tailed pup.
The Bagman taught him many a trick ;
He would carry, and fetch, and run after a stick,

Could well understand
The word of command,
And appear to doze
With a crust on his nose
Till the Bagman permissively waved his hand :
Then to throw up and catch it he never would fail,
As he sat up on end, on his little cock-tail.
Never was puppy so *bien instruit*,
Or possessed of such natural talent as he ;
And as he grew older,
Every beholder
Agreed he grew handsomer, sleeker, and bolder.

Time, however his wheels we may clog,
Wends steadily still with onward jog,
And the cock-tailed puppy's a curly-tailed dog !
When just at the time
He was reaching his prime,
And all thought he'd be turning out something
sublime,
One unlucky day,
How, no one could say,
Whether soft *liaison* induced him to stray,
Or some kidnapping vagabond coaxed him away,
He was lost to the view,
Like the morning dew ;
He had been, and was not—that's all that they
knew.
And the Bagman stormed, and the Bagman swore
As never a Bagman had sworn before ;
But storming or swearing little avails
To recover lost dogs with great curly tails.

(Blogg, the Bagman, subsequently starts for Ostend
on business ; the ship is wrecked, and he is saved by
'a very large, web-footed, curly-tailed dog.'   The
Bagman is thrown on the French coast ; he seeks
shelter at an inn, and goes to bed.)

The dog leaped up, and his paws found a place
On each side his neck in a canine embrace,
And he licked Blogg's hands, and he licked his
    face,
And he waggled his tail as much as to say :
' Mr. Blogg, we 've foregathered before to-day.'
And the Bagman saw, as he now sprang up,
       What, beyond all doubt,
       He might have found out
Before, had he not been so eager to sup,
'Twas Sancho !—the dog he had reared from a
    pup !
The dog who when sinking had seized his hair,—
The dog who had saved, and conducted him
    there,— -
The dog he had lost out of Billiter Square ! !

       *   *   *   *

When abroad, and we have not a single friend
    near,
E'en a cur that will love us becomes very dear,
And the balance of interest 'twixt him and the
    dog,
Of course was inclining to Anthony Blogg,
       Yet he, first of all, ceased
       To encourage the beast,
Perhaps thinking ' Enough is as good as a feast ' ;

And, besides, as we've said, being sleepy and
    mellow,
He grew tired of patting and crying 'Poor
    fellow!'
So his smile by degrees hardened into a frown,
And his 'That's a good dog!' into 'Down,
    Sancho! down!'

But nothing could stop his mute fav'rite's
    caressing,
Who, in fact, seemed resolved to prevent his
    undressing,
        Using paws, tail, and head,
        As if he had said:
'Most beloved of masters, pray, don't go to
    bed;
You had much better sit up, and pat me instead!'
Nay, at last, when determined to take some
    repose,
Blogg threw himself down on the outside the
    clothes,
        Spite of all he could do,
        The dog jumped up too,
And kept him awake with his very cold nose;
        Scratching and whining,
        And moaning and pining,
Till Blogg really believed he must have some
    design in
Thus breaking his rest; above all, when at length
The dog scratched him off from the bed by sheer
    strength.

(The inn-keeper and his friends come quietly into
the room with murderous intent ; a free fight follows.)

   Really, which way
   This desperate fray
Might have ended at last I'm not able to say,
The dog keeping thus the assassins at bay :
But a few fresh arrivals decided the day.

MORAL

And now, gentle reader, before that I say
Farewell for the present, and wish you good-day,
Attend to the moral I draw from my lay.

If ever you travel, like Anthony Blogg,
Be wary of strangers—don't take too much grog !
And don't fall asleep, if you should, like a hog !
Above all—carry with you a curly-tailed dog !

Lastly, don't act like Blogg, who, I say it with
  blushing,
Sold Sancho next month for two guineas at
  Flushing ;
But still on these words of the bard keep a fixed
  eye :
Ingratum si dixeris, omnia dixti !!!

        Barham.

XXVII

ABDIEL

    THE pang
Of famine fed upon all entrails—men
Died, and their bones were tombless as their flesh ;

The meagre by the meagre were devoured,
Even dogs assailed their masters—all save one,
And he was faithful to a corse, and kept
The birds and beasts and famished men at bay,
Till hunger clung them, or the dropping dead
Lured their lank jaws; himself sought out no food,
But with a piteous and perpetual moan,
And a quick desolate cry, licking the hand
Which answered not with a caress—he died.

Byron.

XXVIII

AT THE SIEGE OF CORINTH

HE saw the lean dogs beneath the wall
Hold o'er the dead their carnival,
Gorging and growling o'er carcass and limb;
They were too busy to bark at him!
From a Tartar's skull they had stripped the flesh,
As ye peel the fig when its fruit is fresh;
And their white tusks crunched o'er the whiter
    skull,
As it slipped through their jaws, when their edge
    grew dull,
As they lazily mumbled the bones of the dead,
When they scarce could rise from the spot where
    they fed;
So well had they broken a lingering fast
With those who had fall'n for that night's repast.

Byron.

XXIX

DON JUAN'S SPANIEL

A SMALL old spaniel,—which had been Don Jose's,
   His father's, whom he loved, as ye may think,
For on such things the memory reposes
   With tenderness—stood howling on the brink,
Knowing (dogs have such intellectual noses!),
   No doubt, the vessel was about to sink;
And Juan caught him up, and ere he stepped
Off, threw him in, and after him he leaped.

     *   *   *   *

The fourth day came, but not a breath of air,
   And ocean slumbered like an unweaned child:
The fifth day, and their boat lay floating there;
   The sea and sky were blue, and clear, and mild—
With their one oar (I wish they had had a pair)
   What could they do? And hunger's rage grew
     wild:
So Juan's spaniel, spite of his entreating,
Was killed, and portioned out for present eating.

On the sixth day they fed upon his hide,
   And Juan, who had still refused because
The creature was his father's dog that died,
   Now feeling all the vulture in his jaws,
With some remorse received (though first denied)
   As a great favour one of the fore-paws,
Which he divided with Pedrillo, who
Devoured it, longing for the other too.

                                       Byron.

XXX

ODYSSEUS AND ARGUS

THEN as they spake, upraised his head,
    Pricked up his listening ear,
The dog, whom erst Odysseus bred,
    Old Argus lying near.

He bred him, but his fostering skill
    To himself had naught availed;
For Argus joined not the chase, until
    The King had to Ilion sailed.

To hunt the wild-goat, hart, and hare,
    Him once young huntsmen sped;
But now he lay an outcast there,
Absent his lord, to none a care,
    Upon a dunghill bed.

Where store of dung, profusely flung
    By mules and oxen, lay;
Before the gates it was spread along
    For the hinds to bear away,

As rich manure for the lands they tilled
    Of their prince beyond the sea;
There was Argus stretched, his flesh all filled
    With the dog-worrying flea.

But when by the hound his King was known,
    Wagged was the fawning tail,

Backward his close-clapped ears were thrown,
And up to his master's side had he flown,
   But his limbs he felt to fail.

Odysseus saw, and turned aside
   To wipe away the tear;
From Eumæus he chose his grief to hide,
And 'Strange, passing strange, is the sight,'
     he cried,
   'Of such a dog laid here!

'Noble his shape, but I cannot tell
   If his worth with that shape may suit;
If a hound he be in the chase to excel,
   In fleetness of his foot:

Or worthless as a household hound,
   Whom men by their boards will place,
For no merit of strength or speed renowned
   But admired for shapeless grace.'

'He is the dog of one now dead,
   In a far land away;
But if you had seen,' the swineherd said,
   'This dog in his better day,
When Odysseus hence his warriors led
   To join in the Trojan fray,

'His strength, his plight, his speed so light,
   You had with wonder viewed;
No beast that once had crossed his sight,
   In the depths of the darkest wood,
'Scaped him, as, tracking sure and right,
   He on its trace pursued.

'But now all o'er in sorrows sore
   He pines in piteous wise;
The King upon some distant shore
   In death has closed his eyes;
And the careless women here no more
   Tend Argus as he lies.

'For slaves who find their former lord
   No longer holds the sway
No fitting service will afford,
   Or just obedience pay.

'Far-seeing Jove's resistless power
   Takes half away the soul
From him, who of one servile hour
   Has felt the dire control.'

This said, the swineherd passed the gate,
   And entered the dwelling tall,
Where proud in state the suitors sate
   Within the palace hall.

And darksome death checked Argus' breath
   When he saw his master dear;
For he died his master's eye beneath,
   All in that twentieth year.

Maginn.

XXXI

FELLOWSHIP IN GRIEF

Loved and loving, God her trust,
The shepherd's wife goes dust to dust;

Their dog, his eye half sad, half prompt to save.
Follows the coffin down into the grave.
Behind his man he takes his drooping stand,
The clods jar hollow on the coffin lid :
      Startled, he lifts his head ;
To that quick shudder of his master's pain,
He thrusts his muzzle deep into his hand
      Solicitous, deeper, yet again.

No kind old pressure answers ; shrinking back
Apart, perplexed with broken ties,
Yet loyal, grave-ward down he lies,
His muzzle flat along the snowy track.
The mourners part.   The widowed shepherd goes
Homeward, yet homeless, through the mountain
    snows.
      Him follows slowly, silently,
That dog.   What a strange trouble in his eyes—
      Something beyond relief !
Is it the creature yearning in dumb stress
To burst obstruction up to consciousness,
      And fellowship in reason's grief ?

                      Aird.

XXXII

BETH GELERT

DEEP in the peacefulness of life
   Which breathes amidst these gentle vales,
A little rustic chapel stands,
   And smiles when daylight breaks, or fails.

Its scattered graves in soft moss are arrayed,
   While o'er its head
Paternal mountains hang a loving shade—
   God bless the Dead.

An aged man, a rural lord,
  In old Caernarvonshire,
Lived happy with an only child,
  Beyond all else in nature dear.
Oh, his heart folded round this little child,
   As wall and tower
Of castle-keep, where all beside runs wild,
   Preserve one flower.

In the sweet morning they were seen
  Breasting the mountains, hand in hand ;
Retainers many filled his hall,
  But one was chosen from the band.
His faithful dog, rough Gelert, with them sped,
   Now here !—now there !—
Dashing the dew-drops from the heath-bells red—
   Startling the hare.

When they were tired, and resting sat,
  The shaggy servant stood close by ;
Or bounded off awhile, and showed
  Heart-laughter in activity.
Yet oft returned, and watched with wistful eye
   For pointing hand,
Or look, or tone, that he might rush to obey
   The high command !

He knew all shades of look or mien,
　The varied tone, the sudden glance,
Remembered every spot once seen,
　Though full of mazes as a dance ;
No serious order did he e'er forget,
　　　No loving friend,—
He was as true a heart as could be met
　　　To the world's end.

His valour and his vigilance
　Became a proverb of the vale ;
His instincts made a small romance,
　And shepherd boys preserved each tale ;
His gentleness had all the effect of grace ;
　　　And, for his form,
His only beauty was his honest face—
　　　No common charm.

Somewhat of humour had he, too,
　And oft with head aside
He seemed to meditate on life,—
　Bent his nose down and sighed :
But while men sought his sentiments to scan,
　　　Up looked he brightly—
Barked—wagged his tail—off to the mountains
　ran,
　　　With capers sprightly !

Within the castle, seven years since,
　The old lord's happy child was born,
And Gelert in the castle court
　Drew his first whimpering breath that morn ;

Thus bred, trained, trusted, Gelert and the child
    Romped on the heather,
And 'midst the sunbeams, hail-showers, and
    winds wild
        They played together.

One day this grey lord sat him down
    Upon a hill-side steep,
And brooding o'er past days, his thoughts
    Loosened, and melted into sleep.
The child with Gelert in a pensive mood
        Wandered and strayed
From the hill's foot, and through a neighbouring
    wood
        And its green glade.

The father woke—rose up, and gazed
    On every side, but saw them not ;
The hill descended, searching round,
    But all in vain—he saw them not !
Aloud he called—the mountain echoes called,
        Near and afar !
Homeward he hied, with terrors vague en-
    thralled,
        While rose night's star.

The night-star rose, like a child's clear soul,
    Aloft in the pure serene ;
The father thought, 'Though idly lost,
    By our hall-fire he sits, I ween,'

And fondly hoped that Gelert still had led
       With care discreet,
Had brought safe back, while daylight yet was
    red,
       His wildered feet.

He was not there—had ne'er been seen!
  With lighted brands the throng rush out,
And o'er the hills, vales, wood and glade,
  Their torches flash, their voices shout.
The wild-eyed father led the search all night
       Still, still in vain!
And the first streak of wretched morning light
       Brought maddening pain:

For on the heath there crouched the form
  Of Gelert with a bloody jaw!
He had a grim and anxious look—
  A panting heart, a quivering paw!
His murderous deed they all with horror see—
       The child is dead!
The blood of his sweet playfellow must be
       On Gelert's head.

The shaggy watch-worn face looked up,
  Fraught with pathetic want of speech,
He strove to rise, but down he sank,
  Yet something seemed he to beseech,—
Watching aghast their dreadful looks around.
       They stare, and crowd
Closer and closer on the crouching hound,
       With curses loud!

' Fiend !—fiend !' the father screamed, and rushed
   At Gelert with his iron-capped staff,
And beat his howling skull in twain,
   And stamped him dead with frantic laugh !
The mutilated limbs stretch stiffly out,
      Measuring their grave ;
And then the old man cast himself about,
      Like a burst wave.

' Monster, lie there and rot !' he cried,
   Glaring on Gelert's battered corse,
' Thou wouldst his sure defender be,
   I well believed, whate'er might cross ;
Now hath a heart-damned hunger caused thee
     rend him—
      Oh, help !—none speak—
My dear, lost child—would not kind hand be-
     friend him ?
      Seek with me—seek !'

Slow moved they, searching round about
   And traces soon of blood they found ;
The old man wrung his hands, and cried,
   ' My child lies somewhere on this ground !'
And truly spake he, though in vain dismay,
      For on soft heath,
Embedded and asleep, his darling lay,
      Smiling at death !

The child awoke, and raised himself
   Upon his little hand ;
His rosy cheeks all dimpling smiled
   To see so many round him stand.

The father ran, and, falling on his knees,
    To his breast caught him,
And held him fondly thus with frequent gaze—
    Such bliss it brought him.

' And art thou safe, my little child,
  Sweet flower-bud of my life and hope ?
A minute since my grief ran wild—
  My joy can scarcely now find scope.
I know not if I hold thee safely yet
    And surely here ! '
The child look'd round, then cried with accent shrill,
    ' Where 's Gelert dear ? '

He started up—they followed him,
  When all abruptly they stood fast.
Before them came a frightful dream
  Of struggles fixed—of contest past :
A haggard Snowdon wolf, stark dead and glaring,
    Lay on its back,
Threatening the air—of victory undespairing—
    Ghastly and black !

' Where 's Gelert ? ' cried the child again ;
  And while they stand confounded,
Some peasants bring a mangled shape,
  With heath and grass surrounded.
And two brown paws hang mournfully adown,
    Well known to all,
Which round the child's white neck, so lately
  thrown,
    Fond scenes recall.

The child a loud and wretched wail
   Sent forth, and clasped his hands,
The old man stood all mute and pale,
   He scarcely sees, yet understands ;
Then turns aside his head, and earthward bends
      With close-shut eyes :
'I cannot look on it—I cannot, friends !'
      Moaning he cries.

His followers moved on, bearing still
   The body in their arms ;
The old man led his child along
   Like silence after storms.
Of all the leaden load of grief within
      No word he spake,
But sought atonement for his cruel sin
      Humbly to make.

And in the gentle valley green
   He built a chapel white ;
With simple heart, and mournful mien,
   He said he hoped that he did right.
'The dear remains bring here,' he softly sighed ;
      'In this small space
My once blithe, bounding friend—the castle's
   pride—
      Tenderly place.

'My child's defender here I lay—
   It were a fresh crime not to weep.'
His little child knelt in the clay,
   And said, 'Farewell, dear Gelert—sleep !'

The old man softly stroked his dead friend's breast,
  Sadly, yet bland—
' My faithful, murdered servant, take thy rest—
  Forgive my hand.'

  *   *   *   *

' O, murdered honesty, O friend !
 Destroyed by vengeance blind and wild,
Thou the sure champion to defend—
 Whom first I slew, and then reviled,
 Dumb foster-brother of my child,
Forgive this hand—O, let it make
A resting-place for thy dear sake ;
 So shall this tomb the record hold
  Of thy fair fame,
 While clodded years, in darkness rolled,
  Bury my name.'

        Horne.

XXXIII

GAWAINE AND THE HOUND

' The lady's hound, restore the hound, Sir Knight.'

' The hound,' said Gawaine, much relieved; 'what
 hound ?'
 And then perceived he that the dog he fed,
With grateful steps the kindly guest had found,
 And there stood faithful.—' Friend,' Sir Ga-
 waine said,
' What 's just is just ! the dog must have his due,
The dame had hers, to choose between the two.'

The carle demurred ; but justice was so clear,
　He 'd nought to urge against the equal law ;
He calls the hound, the hound disdains to hear,
　He nears the hound, the hound expands his jaw ;
The fangs were strong and sharp, that jaw within,
The carle drew back—'Sir Knight, I fear you win.'

' My friend,' replies Gawaine, the ever bland
　' I took thy lesson, in return take mine ;
All human ties, alas ! are ropes of sand,
　My lot to-day, to-morrow may be thine ;
But never yet the dog our bounty fed
Betrayed the kindness, or forgot the bread.'

Lytton.

XXXIV

BLOODHOUNDS ON ARTHUR'S TRACK

Then hark again !　The human hunt begun,
　The ringing hoop, the hunter's cheering cry ;
Round and around, by sand, and cave, and steep,
The doubtful ban-dogs, undulating, sweep.

At length, one windeth where the wave hath left
　The unguarded portals of the gorge, and there,
Far-wandering, halts ; and from a rocky cleft,
　Spreads his keen nostril to the whispering air ;
Then, with trailed ears, moves cowering o'er the
　　ground,
The deep bay booming breaks :—the scent is
　　found.

Hound answers hound—along the dank ravine
   Pours the fresh wave of spears and tossing
     plumes;
On—on; and now the idol-shrine obscene
   The dying pine-brand flickeringly illumes;
The dogs go glancing through the shafts of stone,
Trample the altar, hurtle round the throne.

Where the lone priest had watched, they pause
     awhile,
   Then forth, hard-breathing, down the gorge
    they swoop.

      *   *   *   *

Foremost rode Harold, on his mailed breast
   Cranched the strong branches of the groaning
    oak.
Hark, with full peal, as suddenly supprest,
   Behind, the ban-dog's choral joy-cry broke;
Led by the note, he turns him back to reach,
Near the wood's marge, a solitary beech.

Clear space spreads round it for a rood or more;
   Where o'er the space the feathering branches
    bend,
The dogs, wedged close, with jaws that drip with
    gore,
   Growl o'er the carcass of the wolf they rend.
Shamed at their lord's rebuke, they leave the
    feast—
Scent the fresh foot-track of the idol-priest;

And, track by track, deep, deeper through the
    maze,
  Softly they go—the watchful Earl behind.
Here the soft earth a recent hoof betrays ;
  And still a footstep near the hoof they find ;—
So on, so on—the pathway spreads more large,
And daylight rushes on the forest marge.

The dogs bound emulous ; but, snarling, shrink
  Back at the anger of the Earl's quick cry ;—
Near a small water-spring, had paused to drink
  A man half clad, who now, with kindling eye,
And lifted knife, roused by the hostile sounds,
Plants his firm foot, and fronts the glaring hounds.

' Fear not, rude stranger,' quoth the Earl in
    scorn ;
    ' Not thee I seek ; my dogs chase nobler prey.'

The fierce Earl chafed, but longer not delayed ;
  For what he sought the earth itself made plain
In the clear hoof-prints ; to the hounds he
    showed
The clue, and, cheering as they tracked, he rode.

But thrice, to guide his comrades from the maze,
  Rings through the echoing wood his lusty
    horn.
Now o'er waste pastures where the wild bulls
    graze,
  Now labouring up slow-lengthening headlands
    borne,

The steadfast hounds outstrip the horseman's
    flight,
And on the hill's dim summit fade from sight.

But scarcely fade, before, though faint and far,
    Fierce wrathful yells the foe at bay reveal.
On spurs the Saxon, till, like some pale star,
    Gleams on the hill a lance—a helm of steel.

       *   *   *   *

Below the mount, recoiling, circling, move
    The ban-dogs, awed by the majestic rest
Of the great foe ; and, yet with fangs that grin,
And eyes that redden, raves the madding din.

                           Lytton.

XXXV

TOBIAS'S DOG

OF the dog in ancient story
Many a pleasant tale is told ;—
As when young Tobias journeyed
To Ecbatane of old,

By the angel Raphael guided ;
Went the faithful Dog and good,
Bounding through the Tigris meadows
Whilst they fished within the flood ;

Ate the crumbs which at the wedding
Fell upon Raguel's floor ;
Barked for joy to see the cattle
Gathered for the bridal store ;

Barked for joy when young Tobias,
With his bride and all her train,
And the money-bags from Media,
Left for Nineveh again.

And when Anna in the doorway
Stood to watch and wait for him,—
Anxious mother ! waiting, watching,
Till her eyes with tears were dim,—

Saw she not the two men coming,
Young Tobias and his guide,
Hurrying on with their good tidings,
And the Dog was at their side !

They were coming dowered with blessings,
Like the Tigris' boundless flood,
And the Dog with joyous barking
Told the same as best he could.

Mary Howitt.

XXXVI

FLUSH OR FAUNUS

You see this dog ?   It was but yesterday
I mused forgetful of his presence here,
Till thought on thought drew downward tear
    on tear,

When from the pillow, where wet-cheeked I lay,
A head, as hairy as Faunus, thrust its way
Right sudden against my face,—two golden-clear
Great eyes astonished mine,—a drooping ear
Did flap me on either cheek to dry the spray !
I started first, as some Arcadian,
Amazed by goatly god in twilight grove ;
But, as the bearded vision closelier ran
My tears off, I knew Flush, and rose above
Surprise and sadness,—thanking the true Pan,
Who, by low creatures, leads to heights of love.

E. B. Browning.

XXXVII

OLD ROÄ

Naäy, noä mander o' use to be callin' 'im Roä,
   Roä, Roä,
Fo' the dog 's stoän-deäf, an' e 's blind, 'e can
   neither stan nor goä.

But I meäns fur to maäke 'is owd aäge as 'appy
   as iver I can,
Fur I owäs owd Roäver moor nor I iver owäd
   mottal man.

Thou 's rode of 'is back when a babby, afoor thou
   was gotten too owd,
For 'e 'd fetch an' carry like owt, 'e was allus as
   good as gowd.

Eh, but 'e'd fight wi' a will *when* 'e fowt; 'e
    could hold 'is oan,
An' Roä was the dog as knaw'd when an' wheere
    to bury his boane.

An' 'e kep his heäd hoop like a king, an' 'e'd
    niver not down wi' 'is taäil,
Fur 'e'd niver done nowt to be shaämed on, when
    we was i' Howlaby Daäle.

An' 'e sarved me sa well when 'e lived, that, Dick,
    when 'e cooms to be deäd,
I thinks as I'd like fur to hev soom soort of a
    sarvice reäd.

Fur 'e's moor good sense na the Parliament man
    'at stans fur us 'ere,
An' I'd voät fur 'im, my oän sen, if 'e could but
    stan fur the Shere.

'Faäithful an' True'—them words be i' Scriptur
    —an' Faäithful an' True
Ull be fun' upo' four short legs ten times fur one
    upo' two.

An' maäybe they'll walk upo' two, but I knaws
    they runs upo' four,—
Bedtime, Dicky! but waäit till tha 'eärs it be
    strikin' the hour.

Fur I wants to tell tha o' Roä when we lived i'
    Howlaby Daäle.

(The farmer tells how he fell asleep and of what he dreamed. Suddenly, he says :—)

. . . I waäked an' I fun' it was Roäver a-tuggin' an' teärin' my slieäve.

An' I thowt as 'e'd goan cleän-wud, for I noä-
   waeys knaw'd 'is intent ;
An' I says, ' Git awaäy, ya beäst,' an' I fetcht 'im
   a kick an' 'e went.

Then 'e tummled up stairs, fur I 'eärd 'im, as if
   'e'd 'a brokken 'is neck,
An' I'd cleär forgot, little Dicky, thy chaumber
   door wouldn't sneck ;

An' I slep' i' my chair ageën wi' my hairm hingin'
   down to the floor,
An' I thowt it was Roäver a-tuggin' an' tearin' me
   wuss nor afoor,

An' I thowt 'at I kick'd 'im ageän, but I kick'd
   thy moother istead.
' What arta snorin' theere fur ? the house is afire,'
   she said.

*   *   *   *

An' she beäld, ' Ya mun saäve little Dick, an' be
   sharp about it an' all,'
Sa I runs to the yard fur a lether, an' sets 'im
   ageän the wall,

An' I claums an' I mashes the winder hin, when
    I gits to the top,
But the heät drew hout i' my heyes till I feäld
    mysen ready to drop.

Thy moother was howdin' the lether, an' tellin'
    me not to be skeärd,
An' I wasn't afeärd, or I thinks leästwaäys as I
    wasn't afeärd ;

But I couldn't see fur the smoäke wheere thou
    was a-liggin, my lad,
An Roäver was theere i' the chaumber a-yowlin'
    an' yaupin' like mad ;

An' thou was a-beälin' likewise, an' a-squeälin',
    as if tha was bit,
An' it wasn't a bite but a burn, for the mark's o'
    thy shou'der yit ;

Then I call'd out Roä, Roä, Roä, thaw I didn't
    haäfe think as 'e 'd 'ear,
But 'e coom'd thruf the fire wi' my bairn i' 'is
    mouth to the winder theere !

He coom'd like a Hangel o' marcy as soon as 'e
    'eärd 'is naäme,
Or like tother Hangel i' scriptur 'at summun
    seed i' the flaäme,

When summun 'ed hax'd fur a son, an' 'e pro-
    mised a son to she,

An' Roä was as good as the Hangel i' saävin' a
    son fur me.

Sa I browt tha down, an' I says, 'I mun gaw up
    ageën fur Roä.'
'Gaw up ageän fur the varmint?' I tell'd 'er
    'Yeas, I mun goä.'

An' I claumb'd up ageän to the winder, an'
    clemm'd owd Roä by the 'ead,
An' 'is 'air coom'd off i' my 'ands an' I taäked 'im
    at fust for deäd ;

Fur 'e smell'd like a herse a-singein', an' seeäm'd
    as blind as a poop,
An' haäfe on 'im bare as a bublin'. I couldn't
    wakken 'im oop,

But I browt 'im down an' we got to the barn, fur
    the barn wouldn't burn
Wi' the wind blawin' hard tother waäy an' the
    wind wasn't like to turn.

An' I kep a-callin' o' Roä till 'e waggled 'is
    taäil fur a bit . . . .
An' I browt Roä round.

Tennyson.

XXXVIII

TRAY—A HERO

Sing me a hero!   Quench my thirst
Of soul, ye bards!
                    Quoth Bard the first:
' Sir Olaf, the good knight, did don
His helm and eke his habergeon . . .'
Sir Olaf and his bard——!

' That sin-scathed brow' (quoth Bard the second),
' That eye wide ope as though Fate beckoned
My hero to some steep, beneath
Which precipice smiled tempting death . . .'
You too without your host have reckoned!

' A beggar-child' (let's hear this third!)
' Sat on a quay's edge: like a bird
Sang to herself at careless play,
And fell into the stream.   "Dismay!
Help, you the standers-by!"   None stirred.

' Bystanders reason, think of wives
And children ere they risk their lives.
Over the balustrade has bounced
A mere instinctive dog, and pounced
Plumb on the prize.   " How well he dives!

' " Up he comes with the child, see, tight
In mouth, alive too, clutched from quite
A depth of ten feet—twelve, I bet!
Good dog!   What, off again?   There's yet
Another child to save!   All right!

' " How strange we saw no other fall !
It 's instinct in the animal.
Good dog !   But he 's a long while under :
If he got drowned I should not wonder—
Strong current, that against the wall !

' " Here he comes, holds in mouth this time
—What may the thing be?   Well, that 's prime !
Now, did you ever?   Reason reigns
In man alone, since all Tray's pains
Have fished—the child's doll from the slime ! "

' And so, amid the laughter gay,
Trotted my hero off,—old Tray,—
Till somebody, prerogatived
With reason, reasoned : " Why he dived,
His brain would show us, I should say.

' " John, go and catch—or, if needs be,
Purchase—that animal for me !
By vivisection, at expense
Of half-an-hour and eighteenpence,
How brain secretes dog's soul we 'll see ! " '

Robert Browning.

XXXIX

CHARITY'S EYE

ONE evening Jesus lingered in the market-place,
Teaching the people parables of truth and grace,
When in the square remote a crowd was seen to rise,
And stop with loathing gestures and abhorring
      cries.

The Master and His meek disciples went to see
What cause for this commotion and disgust could
be,
And found a poor dead dog beside the gutter
laid—
Revolting sight! at which each face its hate
betrayed.

One held his nose, one shut his eyes, one turned
away,
And all among themselves began to say:
'Detested creature! he pollutes the earth and
air!'
'His eyes are blear!' 'His ears are foul!' 'His
ribs are bare!'

'In his torn hide there's not a decent shoe-
string left,
No doubt the execrable cur was hung for theft!'
Then Jesus spake, and dropped on him this
saving wreath:
'Even pearls are dark before the whiteness of
his teeth.'

The pelting crowd grew silent and ashamed, like
one
Rebuked by sight of wisdom higher than his
own;
And one exclaimed: 'No creature so accursed
can be
But some good thing in him a loving eye will
see.'

Alger.

XL

MERCY'S REWARD

HAST seen
The record written of Salah-ud-Deen
The Sultan—how he met, upon a day,
In his own city on the public way,
A woman whom they led to die ?   The veil
Was stripped from off her weeping face, and
    pale
Her shamed cheeks were, and wild her dark
    fixed eye,
And her lips drawn with terror at the cry
Of the harsh people, and the rugged stones
Borne in their hands to break her, flesh and
    bones ;
For the law stood that sinners such as she
Perish by stoning, and this doom must be ;
So went the wan adult'ress to her death.
High noon it was, and the hot Khamseen's
    breath
Blew from the desert sands and parched the
    town.
The crows gasped, and the kine went up and
    down
With lolling tongues ; the camels moaned ; a
    crowd
Pressed with their pitchers, wrangling high and
    loud,

About the tank; and one dog by a well,
Nigh dead with thirst, lay where he yelped and
　　fell,
Glaring upon the water out of reach,
And praying succour in a silent speech,
So piteous were its eyes.　Which, when she
　　saw,
This woman from her foot her shoe did draw,
Albeit death-sorrowful, and looping up
The long silk of her girdle, made a cup
Of the heel's hollow, and thus let it sink
Until it touched the cool black water's brink;
So filled th' embroidered shoe, and gave a
　　draught
To the spent beast, which whined, and fawned,
　　and quaffed
Her kind gift to the dregs; next licked her
　　hand,
With such glad looks that all might understand
He held his life from her; then, at her feet
He followed close, all down the cruel street,
Her one friend in that city.
　　　　　　　　　　But the King,
Riding within his litter, marked this thing,
And how the woman, on her way to die,
Had such compassion for the misery
Of that parched hound: 'Take off her chain,
　　and place
The veil once more above the sinner's face,
And lead her to her house in peace!' he said.
'The law is that the people stone thee dead

For that which thou hast wrought; but there is
    come,
Fawning around thy feet, a witness dumb,
Not heard upon thy trial; this brute beast
Testifies for thee, sister! whose weak breast
Death could not make ungentle.   I hold rule
In Allah's stead, who is "the Merciful,"
And hope for mercy; therefore go thou free—
I dare not show less pity unto thee!'

      As we forgive—and more than we—
      Ya Barr! good God! show clemency.
                    Sir Edwin Arnold.

XLI

THE SCHOOLMASTER'S STORY

               THE laddie still
Was seated on my knee, when at the door
We heard a sound of scraping: Willie pricked
His ears and listened, then he clapt his hands—
'Hey! Donald, Donald, Donald!'   (See! the
    rogue
Looks up and blinks his eyes—he kens his
    name!)
'Hey! Donald, Donald!' Willie cried.   At that
I saw beneath me, at the door, a Dog—
The very collie dozing at your feet,
His nose between his paws, his eyes half closed.

At sight of Willie, with a joyful bark
He leapt and gambolled, eyeing me the while
In queer suspicion ; and the mannock peeped
Into my face, while patting Donald's back—
' It's Donald ! he has come to take me home ! '
An old man's tale, a tale for men grey-haired,
Who wear, thro' second childhood, to the grave !
I 'll hasten on.   Thenceforward Willie came
Daily to school, and daily to the door
Came Donald trotting ; and they homeward
      went
Together—Willie walking slow but sure,
And Donald trotting sagely by his side.
(Ay, Donald, he is dead ! be still, old man !)

          *   *   *   *

                One day in school I saw,
Through threaded window-panes, soft snowy
      flakes
Fall with unquiet motion, mistily, slowly,
At intervals ; but when the boys were gone,
And in ran Donald with a dripping nose,
The air was clear and grey as glass.   An hour
Sat Willie, Donald, and myself, around
The murmuring fire, and then with tender hand
I wrapt a comforter round Willie's throat,
Buttoned his coat around him close and warm,
And off he ran with Donald, happy-eyed
And merry, leaving fairy prints of feet
Behind him on the snow.   I watched them fade
Round the white curve, and, turning with a sigh,

Came in to sort the room and smoke a pipe
Before the fire.   Here, dreaming all alone,
I sat and smoked, and in the fire saw clear
The norland mountains, white and cold with snow
That crumbled silently, and moved, and changed,—
When suddenly the air grew sick and dark,
And from the distance came a hollow sound,
A murmur like the moan of far-off seas.

Above the moaning of the wind I heard
A sudden scraping at the door ; my heart
Stood still and listened ; and with that there rose
An awesome howl, shrill as a dying screech,
And scrape—scrape—scrape, the sound beyond
        the door !
I could not think—I could not breathe—a dark,
Awful foreboding gript me like a hand,
As opening the door I gazed straight out,
Saw nothing, till I felt against my knees
Something that moved, and heard a moaning
        sound—
Then, panting, moaning, o'er the threshold leapt
Donald the dog, alone, and white with snow.

'Down, Donald ! down, old man !'   Sir, look at
        him !
I swear he knows the meaning of my words,
And tho' he cannot speak, his heart is full !
See now ! see now ! he puts his cold black nose
Into my palm and whines!—he knows! he knows!
Would speak, and cannot, but he minds that night!

The terror of my heart seemed choking me.
Dumbly I stared and wildly at the dog,
Who gazed into my face and whined and moaned,
Leaped at the door, then touched me with his
    paws,
And lastly, gript my coat between his teeth,
And pulled and pulled—whiles growling, whin-
    ing whiles—
Till fairly maddened, in bewildered fear,
I let him drag me through the banging door
Out to the whirling storm.   Bareheaded, wild,
The wind and snow-drift beating on my face,
Blowing me hither, thither, with the dog,
I dashed along the road.   What followed seemed
An eerie, eerie dream !—a world of snow,
A sky of wind, a whirling howling mist
Which swam around with hundred sickly eyes ;
And Donald dragging, dragging, beaten, bruised,
Leading me on to something that I feared—
An awful something, and I knew not what !
On, on, and farther on, and still the snow
Whirling, the tempest moaning !   Then I mind
Of groping blindly in the shadowy light,
And Donald by me burrowing with his nose
And whining.   Next a darkness, blank and deep!
But then I mind of tearing thro' the storm,
Stumbling and tripping, blind and deaf and
    dumb,
And holding to my heart an icy load
I clutched with freezing fingers.

     *   *   *   *

And Willie's dead !—that's all I comprehend—
Ay, bonnie Willie Baird has gone before:
The school, the tempest, and the eerie pain,
Seem but a dream,—and I am weary like.
I begged old Donald hard—they gave him
        me—
And we have lived together in this house,
Long years, with no companions.   There's no
        need
Of speech between us !   Here we dumbly bide,
But ken each other's sorrow,—and we both
Feel weary.   When the nights are long and
        cold,
And snow is falling as it falleth now,
And wintry winds are moaning, here I dream
Of Willie and the unfamiliar life
I left behind me on the norland hills !
' Do doggies gang to heaven ?' Willie asked ;
And ah ! what Solomon of modern days
Can answer that ?   Yet here at nights I sit,
Reading the Book, with Donald at my side ;
And stooping with the Book upon my knee,
I sometimes gaze in Donald's patient eyes—
So sad, so human, though he cannot speak—
And think he knows that Willie is at peace,
Far, far away beyond the norland hills,
Beyond the silence of the untrodden snow.

                              Buchanan.

XLII

TOLD TO THE MISSIONARY

JUST look 'ee here, Mr. Preacher, you 're a-goin' a
    bit too fur ;
There isn't the man as is livin' as I 'd let say a
    word agen her.
She 's a rum-lookin' bitch, that I own to, and
    there *is* a fierce look in her eyes,
But if any cove sez as she 's vicious, I sez in his
    teeth he lies.
Soh ! gently, old 'ooman; come here, now, and
    set by my side on the bed ;
I wonder who 'll have yer, my beauty, when him
    as you 're all to 's dead !
There, stow yer perlaver a minit ; I knows as my
    end is nigh ;
Is a cove to turn round on his dog, like, just 'cos
    he 's goin' to die ?

Oh, of course, I was sartin you 'd say it. It 's
    allus the same with you,
Give it us straight now, guv'nor,—what would
    you have me do ?
Think of my soul ?—I do, sir. Think of my
    Saviour ?—Right !
Don't be afeard of the bitch, sir ; *she 's* not a-
    goin' to bite.

Tell me about my Saviour—tell me that tale
agen,
How he prayed for the coves as killed him, and
died for the worst of men.
It's a tale as I always liked, sir; and bound for
the 'ternal shore,
I thinks it aloud to myself, sir, and I likes it
more and more.

I've thumbed it out in the Bible, and I know it
now by heart,
And it's put like steam in my boiler, and made
me ready to start.
I ain't not afeard to die now; I've been a bit
bad in my day,
But I know when I knock at them portals there's
one as won't say me nay.
And it's thinkin' about that story, and all as he
did for us,
As makes me so fond o' my dawg, sir, specially
now I'm wus;
For a-savin' o' folks who'd kill us is a beautiful
act, the which
I never heard tell on o' no one, 'cept o' him
and o' that there bitch.

*   *   *   *

'Twas five years ago come Chrismus, maybe
you remember the row,
There was scares about hydryphoby—same as
there be just now;

And the bobbies came down on us costers—
    came in a reggerlar wax,
And them as 'ud got no licence was summerned
    to pay the tax.
But I had a friend among 'em, and he come in a
    friendly way,
And he sez, ' You must settle your dawg, Bill,
    unless you 've a mind to pay.'
The missus was dyin' wi' fever—I 'd made a
    mistake in my pitch,
I *couldn't* afford to keep her, so I sez, ' I 'll
    drownd the bitch ! '

I wasn't a-goin' to *lose* her, I warn't such a brute,
    you bet,
As to leave her to die by inches o' hunger, and
    cold, and wet ;
I never said now't to the missus—we both on us
    liked her well—
But I takes her the follerin' Sunday down to the
    Grand Canell.
I gets her tight by the collar—the Lord forgive
    my sin !
And, kneelin' down on the towpath, I ducks the
    poor beast in.
She gave just a sudden whine like, then a look
    comes into her eyes
As 'ull last for ever in mine, sir, up to the day I
    dies.

And a chill came over my heart then, and think-
    in' I heard her moan,

I held her below the water, beating her skull
    with a stone.
You can see the mark of it now, sir—that place
    on the top of 'er 'ed—
And sudden she ceased to struggle, and I fancied
    as she was dead.
I shall never know how it happened, but goin'
    to loose my hold,
My knees slipped over the towpath, and into
    the stream I rolled;
Down like a log I went, sir, and my eyes were
    filled with mud,
And the water was tinged above me with a
    murdered creeter's blood.

I gave myself up for lost then, and I cursed in
    my wild despair,
And sudden I rose to the surfis, and a su'thing
    grabbed my hair—
Grabbed at my hair and loosed it, and grabbed
    me agin by the throat,
And *she* was a-holdin' my 'ed up, and somehow
    I kep' afloat.
I can't tell yer 'ow she done it, for I never
    know'd no more,
Till somebody seized my collar, and giv' me a
    lug ashore;
And my head was queer and dizzy, but I see as
    the bitch was weak,
And she lay on her side a-pantin' waitin' for me
    to speak.

What did I do with *her,* eh? You'd ahardly
    need to ax,
But I sold my barrer a Monday, an' paid the
    bloomin' tax.

That's right, Mr. Preacher, pat her—you ain't
    not afeard of her now !—
Dang this here tellin' o' stories—look at the
    muck on my brow !

I'm weaker, an' weaker, an' weaker; I fancy the
    end ain't fur,
But you know why here on my deathbed I think
    o' the Lord and her,
And he who by men's hands tortured uttered that
    prayer divine,
'Ull pardon me linkin' him like with a dawg as
    forgave like mine.
When the Lord in his mercy calls me to my last
    eternal pitch,
I know as you'll treat her kindly—promise to
    take my bitch !

Sims.

XLIII

MEDIÆVAL METRICAL ROMANCES—I

THE DOG AND THE ADDER

THERE was a knight,
A rich man of great might,

And had a good woman to wife,
And a woman of good life.
Between them there came an heir;
A good child and a fair,
And young age it was,
A twelvemonth old it was.
There was no thing such
That the knight loved so much.
The knight had another jewel
That he loved so well.
A greyhound that was good and snel,
And the knight loved it well.

(The child is left alone one day by its nurses, who are attracted by a tournament outside.)

In the court there was wrought
An old tower that served of nought,
And in a crevice there was bred
An adder, and had therein a bed.
Then the adder woke and heard
All the people how it fared,
Trump, tabor, and melody,
And heraldis loud cry,
The adder sought way over all
Till she came out of the wall.
Out of the wall she came,
Into the hall that way she name,
And drove him toward the cradle near
To slay the child that was there.
Toward the cradle as he did slide,
The good greyhound lay and spied,

And was so wroth withal
That he came into the hall.
The greyhound stood up anon,
And to the adder he 'gan goon ;
There they foughten together long,
And either wounded other strong.
As they foughten, hear ye moun,
The cradle went upside down ;
The cradle upon the pommels stood—
The child had naught but good ;
It no woke, nor it no weep
But all still and sleep.
The greyhound went the worm so nigh
That into the yard the worm did fly ;
The greyhound followed him so fast,
That he slew him at the last.
Then the adder was fall,
The greyhound laid him in the hall,
Evil wounded over all,
And forsooth he lay and yal.

(The jousts finished, the nurses return. They do not
see the baby, but notice that the greyhound is bloody.
To excuse their neglect of the child, they tell their
mistress that the dog in a mad fit has eaten the little
one. Thus the mother to her lord :—)

'Sir,' she said, 'surely,
The child that thou lovedst so dearly
Thy greyhound has waxen wood,
And has eaten him flesh and blood.'
Then was the lord sorry i-nowe ;
In toward the hall he him drowe,

And the lady with him name.
Into the hall soon he came :
The greyhound his lord did spy,
And set both his feet on high
Upon his breast to make solas ;
And the more harm was.
The knight drew out his sword anon,
And smote out the rygge bone.
The knight commanded anon right,
Bear the cradle out of his sight.
There stood a man that was glad
To do that the knight bade,
And bear the cradle out in his arm,
And saw the child had no harm.
In his arm the child he hent,
And into the hall he went,
And said, ' Alas, thy good greyhound !
Here is thy son whole and sound.'
Then they that were in the hall
Hadden great wonder all
That the child alive was,
And said it was a wonder case.
At the last they founden all
How the case was befall,
How the adder was y-slew
That the greyhound had y-drew.
' Alas ! ' quoth the knight tho',
' My good greyhound is a-goo.'
The knight was sorry therefore,
That his greyhound was forlore ;
Into his orchard the way he nome
And to a fish-pool he come,

And for dole of his hound,
He leapt in, and sank to ground.

Unknown.

XLIV

MEDIÆVAL METRICAL ROMANCES—II

MURDER WILL OUT

(Arcadas, King of Aragon, banishes his wife for
alleged unfaithfulness.   She is escorted by Sir Roger,
who is killed by Sir Marrock, the Iago-like steward of
the King.   Queen Margaret escapes.   Sir Roger is
defended unsuccessfully by his dog :—)

TRUELOVE, his hound so good,
Helped his master and by him stood—
        Bitterly he can bite !

His good hound for weal nor woe
Would not from his master go
        But lay licking his woundis,
He meant to have helped him again,
Thereto he did all his main,
        Great kindness is in houndis !
He licked him till he stank,
Then he began and cunning thank
        To make him a pit of stone,
And to bury him was his purpose,
And scraped on him both rind and moss,
        And from him never would gone.

Seven year, so God me save,
Keepèd he his master's grave,
  Till that he waxed old!
Ever on his master's grave he lay,
There might no man get him away,
  For ought that they could do
But if it were once on the day,
He would forth to get his prey,
  And soon again he would go:
Seven year he lived there,
Till it befell against the Yule,
  Upon the first day,
The hound, as the story says,
Ran to the Kingis palace
  Without any more delay;
As the King at the meat was then,
Into the hall the hound can ren
  Among the knightis gay;
All about he can behold,
And when he saw not that he wold,
  He did him fast away;
The hound runneth ever, I wis,
Till he came there his master is,
  He found not that he sought;
The King wondereth in his wede
From where he came and whither he gaed,
  And who him thither brought;
He thought that he had seen him there,
But he wist not when or where.
  Further then said he nought

But fast be-thinketh he him then,
For he thought he should him ken,
    So sitteth he in a thought.
The tother day, on the same wise,
As the King from the board can rise,
    The hound sped not thro' ;
All about the hall he sought,
But at that time he found him nought,
    Then did he him fast to go.
Then said the King that ilk stounde
' Methinketh that was Sir Roger's hound,
    That went with him thro'
When the queen was flemed out of my land.'
' Sir,' they said, ' we understand
    Forsooth that it is so ! '
The King said, ' What may this mean ?
I trow Sir Roger and the queen
    Be comen to this land,
For never since they went, I wis,
Saw I Sir Roger's hound ere this,
    That is wonder tythand ;
When he goeth, pursue him then,
For evermore he will ren
    Till he come there his master is.'
The tother day among them all
To meat as they were sat in hall,
    Sir Marrock was there, fear within, I
      wis;
And the hound would never blin,
But ran about fast within,
    Till he with him meeteth.

He start up, verament,
The steward by the throat he hent,
    The hound wreaked his master's death ;
The stewardis life is lorn,
There was few that rued theron,
    And few for him weepeth.

The greyhound did him soon to go,
When his master's death he had 'venged so
    On him that wrought him train ;
All they followed him in that tide,
Some on horses and some beside,
    Knightis, squires and swain.
Rest would he never have
Till he came to his master's grave,
    And then turned he again ;
They might not get him therefro,
He stood at 'fence against them tho',
    And they would him have slain.
When they saw no better boot,
They turned again on horse and foot,
    With great wonder, I ween.
They told the King all thus :
' Alas !' said King Ardus,
    ' What may this be to mean ?
I trow Sir Marrock, by God's pain,
Have slain Sir Roger by some train,
    And falsely flemed my queen !
The hound had not Sir Marrock slain,
Had not some treason been,
    By dearworth God, as I ween !'

They went again, both knight and knave,
And found Sir Roger in his grave,
    As whole as he was laid.

Sir Roger's corse with no delay
They buried it the other day,
    With many a bold baron;
His hound would not from him away,
But ever on his grave he lay,
    Till death had brought him down.

Unknown.

XLV

DOUBT AS TO IDENTITY

THERE was a little woman, as I 've heard tell,
    She went to market her eggs for to sell,
She went to market all on a market-day,
    And she fell asleep on the king's highway.

By came a pedlar whose name it was Stout,
    He cut her petticoats all round about;
He cut her petticoats up to her knees,
    Which made the little woman to shiver and to
    freeze.

When this little woman began to awake,
    She began to shiver and she began to shake,
She began to shake, and she began to cry,
    Lauk a mercy on me! this is none of I!

If it be I, as I do hope it be,
  I 've a little dog at home, and he knows me ;
If it be I he 'll wag his little tail,
  But if it be not I he 'll bark and wail.

When this little woman went home in the dark,
  Up starts the little dog, and he began to bark ;
He began to bark, so she began to cry,
  Lauk a mercy on me ! this is none of I.

Unknown.

XLVI

THE INDIAN HERO'S CREED

Lo ! suddenly, with a sound which rang through
    heaven and earth,
Indra came riding on his chariot, and he cried to
    the king, ' Ascend ! '
Then, indeed, did the lord of justice look back
    to his fallen brothers,
And thus unto Indra he spoke, with a sorrowful
    heart :
' Let my brothers, who yonder lie fallen, go with
    me ;
Not even unto thy heaven would I enter, if they
    were not there.
And yon fair-faced daughter of a king, Draupadi,
    the all-deserving,
Let her, too, enter with us !   O Indra, approve
    my prayer ! '

INDRA

'In heaven thou shalt find thy brothers,—they
    are already there before thee;
There are they all, with Draupadi; weep not,
    then, O son of Bharata,
Thither are they entered, prince, having thrown
    away their mortal weed;
But thou alone shalt enter still wearing thy body
    of flesh.'

YUDISHTHIRA

'O Indra, and what of this dog?   It hath faith-
    fully followed me through;
Let it go with me into heaven, for my soul is full
    of compassion.'

INDRA

'Immortality and fellowship with me, and the
    height of joy and felicity,
All these hast thou reached to day: leave, then,
    the dog behind thee.'

YUDISHTHIRA

'The good may oft act an evil part, but never a
    part like this;
Away, then, with that felicity whose price is to
    abandon the faithful!'

INDRA

'My heaven hath no place for dogs; they steal
    away our offerings on earth:
Leave, then, thy dog behind thee, nor think in
    thy heart that it is cruel.'

YUDISHTHIRA

'To abandon the faithful and devoted is an end-
less crime, like the murder of a Brahmin;

Never, therefore, come weal or woe, will I abandon
yon faithful dog.

Yon poor creature, in fear and distress, hath
trusted in my power to save it:

Not, therefore, for e'en life itself will I break my
plighted word.'

INDRA

'If a dog but beholds a sacrifice, men esteem it
unholy and void;

Forsake, then, the dog, O hero, and heaven is
thine own as a reward.

Already thou hast borne to forsake thy fondly
loved brothers and Draupadi;

Why, then, forsakest thou not the dog? Where-
fore now fails thy heart?'

YUDISHTHIRA

Mortals, when they are dead, are dead to love or
hate,—so runs the world's belief;

I could not bring them back to life, but while
they lived I never left them.

To oppress the suppliant, to kill a wife, to rob
a Brahmin, and to betray one's friend,

These are the four great crimes; and to forsake
a dependant I count equal to them.'

Unknown.

PART II

SPORTING POEMS

Throw off thy ready pack.   See where they spread,
And range around, and dash the glistening dew.
If some staunch hound with his authentic voice
Avow the recent trail, the jostling tribe
Attend his call, then, with one mutual cry,
The welcome news confirm, and echoing hills
Repeat the pleasing tale.

SOMERVILE.

XLVII

THE FAWNING WHELP

THE master Hunt, anon, foot-hot,
With his horn blew three mote
At the uncoupling of his houndis;
Within a while the hart found is,
Y-halloaed, and rechasèd fast
Long time, and so, at the last,
This hart roused and stole away
From all the hounds a privy way.
The hounds had overshot him all,
And were upon a default y-fall,
Therewith the Hunt wonder fast
Blew a forlorn at the last;
I was go walkèd from my tree,
And, as I went, there came by me
A whelp, that fawned me as I stood,
That had y-followed, and could no good;
It came and crept to me as low
Right as it had me y-know,
Held down his head, and joined his ears,
And laid all smooth down his hairs:
I would have caught it anon,
It fled, and was from me gone.

                                    Chaucer.

XLVIII

LYCURGUS' ALAUNS

About his chair there wenten white alauns,
Twenty and more, as great as any steer,
To hunten at the lion or the deer,
And followed him, with muzzle fast y-bound,
Coloured with gold, and torettes filed around.

Chaucer.

XLIX

THE PROPERTIES OF A GOOD
GREYHOUND

A greyhound should be headed like a Snake,
And necked like a Drake,
Footed like a Cat,
Tailed liked a Rat,
Sidèd like a Team,
Chined like a Beam.

The first year he must learn to feed,
The second year to field him lead,
The third year he is fellow-like,
The fourth year there is none sike,
The fifth year he is good enough,
The sixth year he shall hold the plough,
The seventh year he will avail
Great bitches for to assail,

The eighth year lick ladle,
The ninth year cart saddle,
And when he is comen to that year
Have him to the tanner,
For the best hound that ever bitch had
At nine year he is full bad.

Juliana Berners.

L

SUNDAY BEAR-BAITING

What folly is this, to keep with danger
A great mastiff dog, and a foul ugly bear?
And to this one end, to see them two fight
With terrible tearings—a foul ugly sight.
And yet methinks those men be most fools of all,
Whose store of money is but very small,
And yet every Sunday they will surely spend
One penny or two, the Bearward's living to mend.

At Paris Garden each Sunday a man shall not fail
To find two or three hundred for the Bearward's
    vale.
One halfpenny a piece they use for to give,
When some have not more in their purses, I believe.
Well, at the last day their conscience will declare
That the poor ought to have all that they may
    spare.
If you therefore it give to see a bear-fight,
Be sure God his curse upon you will light.

Crowley.

LI

THE BLAZON PRONOUNCED BY THE HUNTSMAN

I AM the Hunt which rathe and early rise ;
(My bottle filled with wine in any wise)
Two draughts I drink, to stay my steps withal,
For each foot one, because I would not fall ;
Then take my Hound in liam me behind,
The stately Hart, in frith or fell to find.
And while I seek his slot where he hath fed,
The sweet birds sing to cheer my drowsy head.
And when my Hound doth strain upon good vent,
I must confess the same doth me content.
But when I have my coverts walked about,
And harboured fast the Hart from coming out :
Then I return to make a grave report,
Whereas I find th' assembly doth resort.

The dinner done, I go straightway again
Unto my marks and show my Master plain,
Then put my Hound upon the view to draw
And rouse the Hart out of his lair by law.
O gamesters all, a little by your leave,
Can you such joys in trifling games conceive?

Turberville.

LII

THE WOFUL WORDS OF THE HART

METHINKS (cold fear) bids me bide
In thickest tufts of coverts close, and so myself
    to hide.
Ah, rueful remedy so that I (as it were)
Even tear my life out of the teeth of hounds,
    which make me fear,
And from those cruel curs and brain-sick bawling
    tykes,
Which do foot out to follow me both over hedge
    and dykes.

Turberville.

LIII

THE HARE'S COMPLAINT

THE scenting Hounds pursued
    The hasty Hare of foot :
The silly Beast to 'scape the Dogs
    Did jump upon a root.

The rotten scrag it burst,
    From cliff to seas he fell :
Then cried the Hare, ' Unhappy me,
    For now perceive I well

'Both Land and Sea pursue
  And hate the hurtless Hare:
And eke the doggèd skies aloft,
  If so the Dog be there.'

Turberville.

LIV

THE TUMBLER

THE hound that men the Tumbler name,
When he a hare or coney doth espy,
Doth seem another way his course to frame,
As though he meant not to approach more nigh,
But yet he meeteth at the last his game,
And shaketh it until he make it die.

Harington.

LV

GREYHOUND IN SLIP

A GREYHOUND which the hunters hold in slip,
Doth strive to break the string, or slide the
    collar,
(That sees the fearful deer before him skip,
Pursued belike with some Actæon's scholar)
And when he sees he can by no means slip,
Doth howl, and whine, and bites the string for
    choler.

Harington.

LVI

THE COURSING

THE man whose vacant mind prepares him to
    the sport,
The finder sendeth out, to seek out nimble
    Wat,
Which crosseth in the field, each furlong, every
    flat,
Till he this pretty beast upon the form hath
    found,
Then viewing for the course, which is the fairest
    ground,
The greyhounds forth are brought, for coursing
    then in case,
And choicely in the slip, one leading forth a
    brace ;
The finder puts her up, and gives her coursers
    law.
And whilst the eager dogs upon the start do
    draw,
She riseth from her seat, as though on earth she
    flew,
Forced by some yelping cute to give the grey-
    hounds view,
Which are at length let slip, when gunning out
    they go,
As in respect of them the swiftest wind were
    slow,

When each man runs his horse, with fixèd eyes,
    and notes
Which dog first turns the hare, which first the
    other coats,
They wrench her once or twice, e'er she a turn
    will take,
What's offered by the first, the other good doth
    make ;
And turn for turn again with equal speed they
    ply,
Bestirring their swift feet with strange agility :
A hardened ridge or way, when if the hare do
    win,
Then, as shot from a bow, she from the dogs
    doth spin,
That strive to put her off, but when he cannot
    reach her,
This giving him a coat, about again doth fetch
    her
To him that comes behind, which seems the hare
    to bear ;
But with a nimble turn she casts them both
    arrear :
Till oft for want of breath to fall to ground they
    make her,
The greyhounds both so spent that they want
    breath to take her.

Drayton.

LVII

THE MUSIC OF THE HOUNDS

THESEUS

Go, one of you, find out the forester,
For now our observation is performed,
And since we have the vaward of the day,
My love shall hear the music of my hounds :
Uncouple in the western valley ; let them go :—
Despatch, I say, and find the forester.

[Exit an Attendant.

We will, fair queen, up to the mountain's top,
And mark the musical confusion
Of hounds and echo in conjunction.

HIPPOLYTA

I was with Hercules and Cadmus once,
When in a wood of Crete they bayed the bear
With hounds of Sparta : never did I hear
Such gallant chiding ; for, besides the groves,
The skies, the fountains, every region near
Seemed all one mutual cry : I never heard
So musical a discord, such sweet thunder.

THESEUS

My hounds are bred out of the Spartan kind,
So flewed, so sanded ; and their heads are hung
With ears that sweep away the morning dew ;

Crook-kneed, and dew-lapped like Thessalian
　　　bulls ;
Slow in pursuit, but matched in mouth like bells,
Each under each.　A cry more tuneable
Was never hollaed to, nor cheered with horn,
In Crete, in Sparta, nor in Thessaly :
Judge when you hear.

Shakespeare.

LVIII

RIVAL FAVOURITES

LORD

Huntsman, I charge thee, tender well my
　　　hounds :
Trash Merriman,—the poor cur is embossed ;
And couple Clowder with the deep-mouthed
　　　brach.
Saw'st thou not, boy, how Silver made it good
At the hedge-corner, in the coldest fault ?
I would not lose the dog for twenty pound.

HUNTSMAN

Why, Belman is as good as he, my lord ;
He cried upon it at the merest loss,
And twice to-day picked out the dullest scent :
Trust me, I take him for the better dog.

LORD

Thou art a fool : if Echo were as fleet,
I would esteem him worth a dozen such.
But sup them well, and look unto them all :
To-morrow I intend to hunt again.

Shakespeare.

LIX

THE BEAR-BAITING CUR

OFT have I seen a hot o'erweening cur
Run back and bite, because he was withheld ;
Who, being suffered with the bear's fell paw,
Hath clapped his tail between his legs and cried.

Shakespeare.

LX

ROMAN HUNTING

(A forest near Rome.   Horns and cry of hounds
    heard.   Enter TITUS ANDRONICUS, who speaks
    with hunters.)

THE hunt is up, the morn is bright and grey,
The fields are fragrant and the woods are green :
Uncouple here and let us make a bay,
And wake the Emperor and his lovely bride,
And rouse the prince, and ring a hunter's peal,
That all the court may echo with the noise.

(A cry of hounds and horns winded in a peal.
    Enter SATURNINUS, TAMORA, etc.)

Many good-morrows to your majesty ;
Madam, to you as many and as good.
I promised your grace a hunter's peal.

SATURNINUS

Come on, then ; horse and chariots let us have,
And to our sport. (*To* TAMORA) Madam, now
  shall ye see
Our Roman hunting.

MARCUS

            I have dogs, my lord,
Will rouse the proudest panther in the chase,
And climb the highest promontory top.

TITUS

And I have horse will follow where the game
Makes way, and run like swallows o'er the plain.
                        Shakespeare.

LXI

VENUS WITH ADONIS' HOUNDS

By this, she hears the hounds are at a bay ;
Whereat she starts, like one that spies an adder
Wreathed up in fatal folds just in his way,
The fear whereof doth make him shake and
  shudder,
  Even so the timorous yelping of the hounds
  Appals her senses and her spright confounds.

For now she knows it is no gentle chase,
But the blunt boar, rough bear, or lion proud,
Because the cry remaineth in one place,
Where fearfully the dogs exclaim aloud :
    Finding their enemy to be so cursed
    They all strain courtesy who shall cope him first.

    *   *   *   *

Here kennelled in a brake she finds a hound,
And asks the weary caitiff for his master,
And there another licking of his wound,
'Gainst venomed sores the only sovereign plaster
    And here she meets another sadly scowling,
    To whom she speaks, and he replies with
        howling.

When he hath ceased his ill-resounding noise,
Another flap-mouthed mourner, black and grim,
Against the welkin volleys out his voice ;
Another and another answer him,
    Clapping their proud tails to the ground below,
    Shaking their scratched ears, bleeding as
        they go.

Shakespeare.

LXII

THE LOMBARD STAG-HUNT

CHEERED as the woods (where new waked choirs
    they meet)
Are all ; and now dispose their choice relays

Of horse and hounds, each like each other fleet ;
Which best, when with themselves compared,
    we praise.

To them old forest spies, the harbourers,
With haste approach, wet as still weeping night,
Or deer that mourn their growth of head with
    tears,
When the defenceless weight does hinder flight.

And dogs, such whose cold secrecy was meant
By Nature for surprise, on these attend ;
Wise temp'rate lime-hounds that proclaim no
    scent,
Nor harb'ring will their mouths in boasting spend.

Yet vainlier far than traitors boast their prize,
(On which their vehemence vast rates does lay,
Since in that worth their treason's credit lies)
These harb'rers praise that which they now be-
    tray.

Boast they have lodged a stag, that all the race
Out-runs of Croton horse, or Regian hounds ;
A stag made long since royal in the chase,
If kings can honour give by giving wounds.

       *   *   *   *

But now, as his last remedy to live,
(For ev'ry shift for life kind Nature makes,
Since life the utmost is which she can give)
Cool Adige from the swoln bank he takes.

But this fresh bath the dogs will make him
    leave,
Whom he sure nosed as fasting tigers found;
Their scent no north-east wind could e'er de-
    ceive
Which drives the air, nor flocks that foul the
    ground.

Swift here the flyers and pursuers seem;
The frighted fish swim from their Adige,
The dogs pursue the deer, he the fleet stream,
And that hastes too to th' Adriatic sea.

Refreshed thus in this fleeting element,
He up the steadfast shore did boldly rise;
And soon escaped their view, but not their
    scent,
That faithful guide, which even conducts their
    eyes.

      *   . *   *   *

For on the shore the hunters him attend;
And whilst the chase grew warm as is the day,
(Which now from the hot zenith does descend)
He is embossed, and wearied to a bay.

Yet life he so esteems, that he allows
It all defence his force and rage can make;
And to the eager dogs such fury shows,
As their last blood some unrevenged forsake.

                           Davenant.

LXIII

BEAR-BAITING

But now a sport more formidable
Had raked together village rabble;
'Twas an old way of recreating,
Which learnèd butchers call bear-baiting.
A bold adventurous exercise
With ancient heroes in high prize,
For authors do affirm it came
From Isthmian and Nemæan game:
Others derive it from the Bear
That's fixed in northern hemisphere,
And round about the pole does make
A circle, like a bear at stake.

We read, in Nero's time, the Heathen
When they destroyed the Christian brethren,
They sewed them in the skins of bears,
And then set dogs about their ears;
From whence, no doubt, th' invention came
Of this lewd anti-christian game.

*   *   *   *

So lawyers lest the bear defendant
And plaintiff dog should make an end on't,
Do stave and tail with writs of error,
Reverse of judgment and demurrer,
To let them breathe a while, and then
Cry whoop, and set them on again.

Butler.

LXIV

THE USES OF THE DOG

Nor last, forget thy faithful dogs; but feed
With fattening whey the mastiff's generous breed,
And Spartan race; who, for the fold's relief,
Will prosecute with cries the nightly thief;
Repulse the prowling wolf, and hold at bay
The mountain robbers, rushing to the prey;
With cries of hounds thou may'st pursue the fear
Of flying hares, and chase the fallow deer;
Rouse from their desert dens the bristled rage
Of boars, and beamy stags in toils engage.

Dryden (VIRGIL).

LXV

PROCRIS' IMMORTAL LELAPS

CEPHALUS' STORY

But with herself she kindly did confer
What gifts the goddess had bestowed on her;
The fleetest greyhound, with this lovely dart,
And I of both have wonders to impart.
Near Thebes a savage beast, of race unknown,
Laid waste the field, and bore the vineyards down;

The swains fled from him, and with one consent
Our Grecian youth to chase the monster went;
More swift than lightning he the toils surpast,
And in his course spears, men, and trees o'ercast.
We slipt our dogs, and last my Lelaps too,
When none of all the mortal race would do:
He long before was struggling from my hands,
And, ere we could unloose him, broke his bands,
That minute where he was, we could not find,
And only saw the dust he left behind.
I climbed a neighbouring hill to view the chase,
While in the plain they held an equal race;
The savage now seems caught, and now by force
To quit himself, nor holds the same straight
    course;
But running counter, from the foe withdraws,
And with short turning cheats his gaping jaws:
Which he retrieves, and still so closely prest,
You'd fear at every stretch he were possessed:
Yet for the gripe his fangs in vain prepare;
The game shoots from him, and he chops the air,
To cast my jav'lin then I took my stand;
But as the thongs were fitting to my hand,
While to the valley I o'erlooked the wood,
Before my eyes two marble statues stood;
That, as pursued appearing at full stretch,
This, barking after, and at point to catch:
Some god their course did with this wonder grace,
That neither might be conquered in the chase.

Tate (OVID).

BONNY HECK

ALAS, alas, quo' bonny Heck
On former days when I reflect !
I was a dog much in respect
    For doughty deed :
But now I must hing by the neck
    Without remeed.

O fy, sirs, for black burning shame,
Ye 'll bring a blunder on your name
Pray tell me wherein I 'm to blame ?
    Is 't, in effect,
Because I 'm cripple, auld and lame ?
    Quo' bonny Heck.

What great feats I have done my sell
Within clink of Kilrenny Bell,
When I was souple, young and fell
    But fear or dread :
John, Ness, and Paterson can tell,
    Whose hearts may bleid.

They 'll witness that I was the vier
Of all the dogs within the shire,
I 'd run all day and never tire :
    But now my neck,
It must be stretchèd for my hire,
    Quo' bonny Heck.

How nimbly could I turn the hare,
Then serve myself, that was right fair!
For still it was my constant care
      The van to lead.
Now, what could sery Heck do mair,
      Syne kill her dead?

At the King's-Muir, and Kelly-law,
Where good stout hares gang fast awa',
So cliverly I did it claw,
      With pith and speed:
I bure the bell before them
      As clear's a beid.

I ran alike on a' kind grounds,
Yea in the midst of Ardry Whines,
I grip't the mackings be the bunns,
      Or be the neck:
Where nathing could slay them but guns,
      Save bonny Heck:

I wily, witty was, and gash,
With my auld felni packy pash,
Nae man might anes buy me for cash
      In some respect.
Are they not then confounded rash,
      That hangs poor Heck?

I was a bardy tyke and bauld,
Tho' my beard's grey, I'm not so auld.

Can any man to me unfald
    What is the feid,
To stane me ere I be well cauld?
    A cruel deed!

Now honesty was ay my drift,
An innocent and harmless shift,
A kaill-pot-lid gently to lift,
    Or amry-sneck.
Shame fa the chafts, dare call that thift,
    Quo' bonny Heck.

So well's I cou'd play hocus pocus,
And of the servants mack jodocus,
And this I did in every locus
    Throw their neglect.
And was not this a merry jocus,
    Quo' bonny Heck?

But now, good sirs, this day is lost,
The best dog in the east-nook coast:
For never ane durst brag nor boast
    Me, for their neck.
But now I must yield up the ghost,
    Quo' bonny Heck.

And put a period to my talking,
For I'm unto my exit making:
Sirs, ye may a' gae to the hawking,
    And there reflect,
Ye'll ne'er get sick a dog for makin'
    As bonny Heck.

But if my puppies ance were ready,
Which I gat on a bonny lady :
They 'll be baith cliver, keen, and beddy,
    And ne'er neglect,
To clink it like their ancient deddy,
      The famous Heck.

William Hamilton.

LXVII

ACTÆON AND HIS HOUNDS

' TELL, if thou canst, the wondrous sight disclosed ;
A goddess naked to thy view exposed.'
This said, the man began to disappear
By slow degrees, and ended in a deer.

As he thus ponders, he behind him spies
His opening hounds, and now he hears their cries :
A generous pack, or to maintain the chase,
Or snuff the vapour from the scented grass.
He bounded off with fear, and swiftly ran
O'er craggy mountains, and the flowery plain ;
Through brakes and thickets forced his way and
    flew
Through many a ring, where once he did pursue.
In vain he oft endeavoured to proclaim
His new misfortune, and to tell his name ;
Nor voice nor words the brutal tongue supplies,
From shouting men, and horns, and dogs, he flies,

Deafened and stunned with their promiscuous
    cries.
When now the fleetest of the pack, that prest
Close at his heels, and sprung before the rest,
Had fastened on him, straight another pair
Hung on his wounded haunch, and held him there,
Till all the pack came up, and every hound
Tore the sad huntsman grovelling on the ground,
Who now appeared but one continued wound.
With dropping tears his bitter fate he moans,
And fills the mountains with his dying groans.
His servants with a piteous look he spies,
And turns about with supplicating eyes.
His servants, ignorant of what had chanced,
With eager haste and joyful shouts advanced,
And called their lord Actæon to the game,
He shook his head in answer to the name;
He heard, but wished he had indeed been gone,
Or only to have stood a looker on.
But, to his grief, he finds himself too near,
And feels his ravenous dogs with fury tear
Their wretched master panting in a deer.

                    Addison (OVID).

LXVIII

A FRAGMENT ON HUNTING-DOGS

THY care be first the various gifts to trace,
The minds and genius of the latrant race.

In powers distinct the different clans excel,
In sight, or swiftness, or sagacious smell.
By wiles ungen'rous some surprise the prey,
And some by courage win the doubtful day.
Seest thou the gazehound how with glance severe
From the close herd he marks the destined deer;
How ev'ry nerve the greyhound's stretch displays,
The hare preventing in her airy maze;
The luckless prey how treach'rous tumblers gain,
And dauntless wolf-dogs shake the lion's mane;
O'er all the bloodhound boasts superior skill
To scent, to view, to turn, and boldly kill,
His fellows' vain alarms rejects with scorn,
True to his master's voice and learned horn:
His nostrils oft, if ancient fame sing true,
Trace the sly felon thro' the tainted dew;
Once snuffed he follows with unaltered aim,
Nor odours lure him from the chosen game;
Deep-mouthed he thunders, and inflamed he
    views,
Springs on relentless, and to death pursues.

     *   *   *   *

   Some hounds of manners vile (nor less we find
Of fops in hounds than in the reas'ning kind)
Puffed with conceit run gadding o'er the plain,
And from the scent divert the wiser train,
For the foe's footsteps fondly snuff their own,
And mar the music with their senseless tone,
Start at the starting prey or rustling wind,
And, hot at first, inglorious lag behind.

Dost thou in hounds aspire to deathless fame?
Learn well their lineage and their ancient stem.
Each tribe with joy old rustic heralds trace,
And sing the chosen worthies of their race.
How his sire's features in the son were spied
When Di was made the vig'rous Ringwood's
    bride.
Less sure thick lips the fate of Austria doom,
Or eagle noses ruled almighty Rome.
Good shape to various kinds old bards confine—
Some praise the Greek and some the Roman
    line:
And dogs to beauty make as diff'ring claims
As Albion's nymphs and India's jetty dames.
Immense to name their lands, to mark their
    bounds,
And paint the thousand families of hounds.

Such be the dog I charge thou mean'st to train:
His back is crooked and his belly plain,
Of fillet stretched, and huge of haunch behind,
A tap'ring tail that nimbly cuts the wind,
Truss thighed, straight hammed, and fox-like
    formed his paw,
Large legged, dry soled, and of protended claw;
His flat wide nostrils snuff the sav'ry steam,
And from his eyes he shoots pernicious gleam;
Middling his head, and prone to earth his view,
With ears and chest that dash the morning dew:
He best to stem the flood, to leap the bound,
And charm the Dryads with his voice profound.

And now thy female bears in ample womb
The bane of hares, and triumphs yet to come,
No sport I ween, nor blast of sprightly horn,
Should tempt me then to hurt the whelps un-
    born.
Unlocked in covers, let her freely run
To range thy courts and bask before the sun.
Near thy full table let the fav'rite stand,
Stroked by thy son's or blooming daughter's
    hand.
Caress, indulge, by arts the matron bribe
T' improve her breed and teem a vig'rous tribe.

Tickell.

LXIX

THE DOGS ON STRIKE

' Let each his discontent reveal :
To yon sour dog I first appeal.'

  ' Hard is my lot,' the hound replies ;
' On what fleet nerves the greyhound flies !
While I, with weary steps and slow,
O'er plains and vales and mountains go :
The morning sees my chase begun,
Nor ends it till the setting sun.'

  ' When,' says the greyhound, ' I pursue,
My game is lost, or caught in view ;

Beyond my sight the prey's secure :
The hound is slow but always sure.
And had I his sagacious scent,
Jove ne'er had heard my discontent.'

Gay.

LXX

BABBLING RINGWOOD

THE morning wakes; the Huntsman sounds,
At once rush forth the joyful hounds;
They seek the wood with eager pace,
Through bush, through brier, explore the chase :
Now scattered wide, they try the plain,
And snuff the dewy turf in vain.
What care, what industry, what pains !
What universal silence reigns !
   Ringwood, a dog of little fame,
Young, pert, and ignorant of game,
At once displays his babbling throat ;
The pack, regardless of the note,
Pursue the scent ; with louder strain
He still persists to vex the train.
   The Huntsman to the clamour flies,
The smacking lash he smartly plies.
His ribs all welked, with howling tone
The Puppy thus expressed his moan :
   ' I know the music of my tongue
Long since the pack with envy stung.

What will not spite? These bitter smarts
I owe to my superior parts.'
   'When puppies prate,' the Huntsman cried,
'They show both ignorance and pride:
Had not thy forward busy tongue
Proclaimed thee always in the wrong,
Thou mightst have mingled with the rest,
And ne'er thy foolish nose confessed.'

Gay.

LXXI

PLAIN WORDS TO THE SPANIEL

The ranging Dog the stubble tries,
And searches every breeze that flies;
The scent grows warm: with cautious fear
He creeps, and points the covey near;
The men in silence, far behind,
Conscious of game, the net unbind.
   A Partridge, with experience wise,
The fraudful preparation spies:
But ere her certain wing she tries
Thus to the creeping Spaniel cries:—
   'Thou fawning slave to man's deceit,
Thou pimp of luxury, sneaking cheat,
Of thy whole species thou disgrace,
Dogs should disown thee of their race!
For if I judge their native parts,
They're born with honest, open hearts;
And ere they served man's wicked ends
Were generous foes, or real friends.'

When thus the Dog with scornful smile :—
'Secure of wing thou dar'st revile. . . .
Thus trained by man, I learned his ways ;
And growing favour feasts my days.'
   ' I might have guessed,' the Partridge said,
' The place where you were trained and fed ;
Servants are apt, and in a trice
Ape to a hair their master's vice.'

Gay.

LXXII

RURAL SPORTS

YET if for sylvan sports thy bosom glow,
Let thy fleet greyhound urge his flying foe.
With what delight the rapid course I view !
How does my eye the circling race pursue !
He snaps deceitful air with empty jaws,
The subtle hare darts swift beneath his paws ;
She flies, she stretches, now with nimble bound
Eager he presses on, but overshoots his ground :
She turns, he winds, and soon regains the way,
Then tears with gory mouth the screaming prey.

See how the well-taught pointer leads the way :
The scent grows warm ; he stops ; he springs
      the prey ;
The fluttering coveys from the stubble rise,
And on swift wing divide the sounding skies ;
The scattering lead pursues the certain sight,
And death in thunder overtakes their flight.

Nor less the spaniel, skilful to betray,
Rewards the fowler with the feathered prey.
Soon as the labouring horse with swelling veins
Hath safely housed the farmer's doubtful gains,
To sweet repast th' unwary partridge flies,
With joy amid the scattered harvest lies;
Wandering in plenty, danger he forgets,
Nor dreads the slavery of entangling nets.
The subtle dog scours with sagacious nose
Along the field, and snuffs each breeze that blows;
Against the wind he takes his prudent way,
While the strong gale directs him to the prey.
Now the warm scent assures the covey near,
He treads with caution, and he points with fear:
Then (lest some sentry fowl the fraud descry,
And bid his fellows from the danger fly)
Close to the ground in expectation lies,
Till in the snare the fluttering covey rise.

Gay.

LXXIII

THE CHASE

THE KENNEL

First let the kennel be the huntsman's care,
Upon some little eminence erect,
And fronting to the ruddy dawn; its courts
On either hand wide opening to receive

The sun's all-cheering beams, when mild he shines,
And gilds the mountain-tops.   For much the pack
(Roused from their dark alcoves) delight to stretch
And bask in his invigorating ray.

Let no Corinthian pillars prop the dome,
A vain expense, on charitable deeds
Better disposed. . . . For use, not state,
Gracefully plain, let each apartment rise.
O'er all let cleanliness preside, no scraps
Bestrew the pavement, and no half-picked bones.

Water and shade no less demand thy care;
In a large square th' adjacent field enclose;
There plant in equal ranks the spreading elm,
Or fragrant lime: most happy thy design
If at the bottom of thy spacious court,
A large canal, fed by the crystal brook,
From its transparent bosom shall reflect
Downward thy structure and inverted grove.

PERFECTION IN THE PACK

A different hound for every different chase
Select with judgment; nor the timorous hare
O'ermatched destroy, but leave that vile offence
To the mean, murderous, coursing crew; intent
On blood and spoil.   O blast their hopes, just
          Heaven !
And all their painful drudgeries repay
With disappointment and severe remorse.

But husband thou thy pleasures, and give scope
To all her subtle play : by Nature led,
A thousand shifts she tries ; t' unravel these
Th' industrious beagle twists his wavering tail,
Through all her labyrinths pursues, and rings
Her doleful knell.   See there with countenance
    blithe,
And with a courtly grin, the fawning hound
Salutes thee cowering, his wide opening nose
Upward he curls, and his large sloe-black eyes
Melt in soft blandishments, and humble joy !
His glossy skin, or yellow-pied, or blue,
In lights or shades by Nature's pencil drawn,
Reflects the various tints : his ears and legs
Flecked here and there, in gay enamelled pride,
Rival the speckled pard ; his rush-grown tail
O'er his broad back bends in an ample arch ;
On shoulders clean, upright, and firm he stands,
His round cat foot, strait hams, and wide-spread
    thighs,
And his low dropping chest, confess his speed,
His strength, his wind, or on the steepy hill,
Or far-extended plain ; in every part
So well proportioned that the nicer skill
Of Phidias himself can't blame thy choice.
Of such compose thy pack.   But here a mean
Observe, nor the large hound prefer, of size
Gigantic ; he in the thick woven covert
Painfully tugs, or in the thorny brake
Torn and embarrassed ; but, if too small,
The pigmy brood in every furrow swims ;

Moiled in the clogging clay, panting they lag
Behind inglorious; or else shivering creep
Benumbed and faint beneath the sheltering thorn.
For hounds of middle size, active and strong,
Will better answer all thy various ends,
And crown thy pleasing labours with success.

But above all take heed, nor mix thy hounds
Of different kinds; discordant sounds shall grate
Thy ears offended, and a lagging line
Of babbling curs disgrace thy broken pack.

THE BLOODHOUND'S SENSE

If the harmonious thunder of the field
Delight thy ravished ears, the deep-flewed hound
Breed up with care, strong, heavy, slow, but sure;
Whose ears, down-hanging from his thick round
    head,
Shall sweep the morning dew, whose clanging
    voice
Awake the mountain echo in her cell,
And shake the forests; the bold Talbot kind
Of these the prime; as white as Alpine snows,
And great their use of old.

Soon the sagacious brute, his curling tail
Flourished in air, low bending plies around
His busy nose, the steaming vapour snuffs
Inquisitive, nor leaves one turf untried,
Till, conscious of the recent stains, his heart
Beats quick; his snuffling nose, his active tail,

Attest his joy; then, with deep opening mouth
That makes the welkin tremble, he proclaims
Th' audacious felon; foot by foot he marks
His winding way, while all the listening crowd
Applaud his reasonings.　O'er the watery ford,
Dry sandy heaths, and stony barren hills,
O'er beaten paths, with men and beasts distained,
Unerring he pursues; till at the cot
Arrived, and seizing by his guilty throat
The caitiff vile, redeems the captive prey:
So exquisitely delicate his sense!

STARTING THE HOUNDS

From the kennel rush the joyous pack;
A thousand wanton gaieties express
Their inward ecstasy, their pleasing sport
Once more indulged, and liberty restored.
The rising sun, that o'er th' horizon peeps,
As many colours from their glossy skins
Beaming reflects, as paints the various bow
When April showers descend.

Huntsman, lead on! behind the clustering pack
Submiss attend, hear with respect thy whip
Loud clanging, and thy harsher voice obey:
Spare not the straggling cur that wildly roves,
But let thy brisk assistant on his back
Imprint thy just resentments; let each lash
Bite to the quick, till howling he return,
And whining creep amid the trembling crowd.

Throw off thy ready pack.   See where they spread,
And range around, and dash the glistening dew.
If some staunch hound with his authentic voice
Avow the recent trail, the jostling tribe
Attend his call, then, with one mutual cry,
The welcome news confirm, and echoing hills
Repeat the pleasing tale.   See how they thread
The brakes, and up yon furrow drive along!
But quick they back recoil, and wisely check
Their eager haste; then o'er the fallowed ground
How leisurely they work, and many a pause
Th' harmonious concert breaks; till more assured
With joy redoubled the low valleys ring.

Happy the man who with unrivalled speed
Can pass his fellows, and with pleasure view
The struggling pack: how in the rapid course
Alternate they preside, and jostling push
To guide the dubious scent; how giddy youth
Oft babbling errs, by wiser age reproved;
How, niggard of his strength, the wise old hound
Hangs in the rear till some important point
Rouse all his diligence, or till the chase
Sinking he finds—then to the head he springs
With thirst of glory fired, and wins the prize.

THE UNHAPPY HARE

And now in open view
See, see, she flies!   Each eager hound exerts
His utmost speed, and stretches every nerve.

How quick she turns—their gaping jaws eludes,
And yet a moment lives ; till, round enclosed
By all the greedy pack, with infant screams
She yields her breath, and there reluctant dies.

A STAG AT BAY

In vain the crowding pack
Draw on the margin of the stream, or cut
The liquid wave with oary feet that move
In equal time.   The gliding waters leave
No trace behind, and his contracted pores
But sparingly perspire : the huntsman strains
His labouring lungs, and puffs his cheeks in vain.
At length a bloodhound bold, studious to kill,
And exquisite of sense, winds him from far ;
Headlong he leaps into the flood, his mouth
Loud opening spends amain, and his wide throat
Swells every note with joy ; then fearless dives
Beneath the wave, hangs on his haunch, and
        wounds
Th' unhappy brute, that flounders in the stream.
Sorely distressed, and struggling strives to mount
The steepy shore.   Haply once more escaped
Again he stands at bay, amid the groves
Of willows, bending low their downy heads.
Outrageous transport fires the greedy pack ;
These swim the deep, and those crawl up with pain
The slippery bank, while others on firm land
Engage ; the stag repels each bold assault,
Maintains his post, and wounds for wounds
        returns.

DEATH OF THE OTTER

Now on firm land they range; then in the flood
They plunge tumultuous; or through reedy pools
Rustling they work their way: no hole escapes
Their curious search. . . . Yon hollow trunk,
That with its hoary head incurved salutes
The passing wave, must be the tyrant's fort
And dread abode.   How these impatient climb,
While others at the root incessant bay!
They put him down.   See, there he dives along!
Th' ascending bubbles mark his gloomy way. . . .
See, that bold hound has seized him; down they sink
Together lost: but soon shall he repent
His rash assault. . . . Again he vents;
Again the crowd attack.   That spear has pierced
His neck. . . . Lo! to yon sedgy bank
He creeps disconsolate: his numerous foes
Surround him, hounds and men.   Pierced
    through and through,
On pointed spears they lift him high in air.

PAIRING TIME

For every longing dame select
Some happy paramour; to him alone
In leagues connubial join.   Consider well
His lineage; what his fathers did of old,
Chiefs of the pack, and first to climb the rock,
Or plunge into the deep, or tread the brake
With thorn sharp-pointed, plashed, and briars
    inwoven.

Observe with care his shape, sort, colour, size.
Nor will sagacious huntsmen less regard
His inward habits.   The vain babbler shun,
Ever loquacious, ever in the wrong.
His foolish offspring shall offend thy ears
With false alarms, and loud impertinence.
Nor less the shifting cur avoid, that breaks
Illusive from the pack; to the next hedge
Devious he strays, there every muse he tries:
If haply then he cross the steaming scent,
Away he flies vain-glorious; and exults
As of the pack supreme, and in his speed
And strength unrivalled.   Lo! cast far behind
His vexed associates pant, and labouring strain
To climb the steep ascent.   Soon as they reach
Th' insulting boaster, his false courage fails,
Behind he lags, doomed to the fatal noose,
His master's hate, and scorn of all the field.
What can from such be hoped, but a base brood
Of coward curs, a frantic vagrant race?

THE LITTER

              Soon as the tender dam
Has formed them with her tongue, with pleasure
      view
The marks of their renowned progenitors,
Sure pledge of triumphs yet to come.   All these
Select with joy; but to the merciless flood
Expose the dwindling refuse, nor o'erload
Th' indulgent mother.   If thy heart relent,

Unwilling to destroy, a nurse provide,
And to the foster parent give the care
Of thy superfluous brood; she'll cherish kind
The alien offspring; pleased thou shalt behold
Her tenderness and hospitable love.
If frolic now and playful they desert
Their gloomy cell, and on the verdant turf,
With nerves improved, pursue the mimic chase,
Coursing around; unto the choicest friends
Commit thy valued prize: the rustic dames
Shall at thy kennel wait, and in their laps
Receive thy growing hopes, with many a kiss
Caress, and dignify their little charge
With some great title, and resounding name
Of high import.

TRAINING THE PUPPIES

But cautious here observe
To check their youthful ardour, nor permit
The inexperienced younker, immature,
Alone to range the woods, or haunt the brakes
Where dodging conies sport—his nerves un-
  strung,
And strength unequal; the laborious chase
Shall stint his growth, and his rash, forward
  youth
Contract such vicious habits, as thy care
And late correction never shall reclaim.

When to full strength arrived, mature and bold,
Conduct them to the field; not all at once,

But as thy cooler prudence shall direct,
Select a few, and form them by degrees
To stricter discipline.   With these consort
The staunch and steady sages of thy pack,
By long experience versed in all the wiles
And subtle doublings of the various chase.
Easy the lesson of the youthful train
When instinct prompts, and when example guides.
If the too forward younker at the head
Press boldly on in wanton sportive mood,
Correct his haste, and let him feel abashed
The ruling whip.   But if he stoop behind
In wary modest guide, to his own nose
Confiding sure, give him full scope to work
His winding way, and with thy voice applaud
His patience and his care; soon shalt thou view
The hopeful pupil leader of his tribe,
And all the listening pack attend his call.

A CURE FOR SHEEP WORRYING

Oft lead them forth where wanton lambkins
      play,
And bleating dams with jealous eyes observe
Their tender care.   If at the crowding flock
He bay presumptuous, or with eager haste
Pursue them scattered o'er the verdant plain—
In the foul fact attached, to the strong ram
Tie fast the rash offender.   See! at first
His horned companion, fearful and amazed,
Shall drag him trembling o'er the rugged ground;

Then, with his load fatigued, shall turn a-head,
And with his hard curled front incessant peal
The panting wretch; till, breathless and astunned,
Stretched on the turf he lie. Then spare not
     thou
The twining whip, but ply his bleeding sides.

VALUABLE VETERANS

Nor is 't enough to breed ; but to preserve
Must be the huntsman's care. The staunch old
     hounds,
Guides of thy pack, though but in number few,
Are yet of great account ; shall oft untie
The Gordian knot, when reason at a stand
Puzzling is lost, and all thy art is vain.
O'er clogging fallows, o'er dry plastered roads,
O'er floated meads, o'er plains with flocks dis-
     tained
Rank-scenting, these must lead the dubious way.

                    Now grown stiff with age,
And many a painful chase, the wise old hound,
Regardless of the frolic pack, attends
His master's side, or slumbers at his ease
Beneath the bending shade ; there many a ring
Runs o'er in dreams ; now on the doubtful soil
Puzzles perplexed, or doubles intricate
Cautious unfolds, then, winged with all his speed,
Bounds o'er the lawn to seize his panting prey ;
And in imperfect whimperings speaks his joy.

APOSTROPHE TO ARGUS

Unnumbered accidents and various ills
Attend thy pack, hang hovering o'er their
　　heads,
And point the way that leads to death's dark
　　cave.
Short is their span ; few at the date arrive
Of ancient Argus, in old Homer's song
So highly honoured—kind, sagacious brute !
Not ev'n Minerva's wisdom could conceal
Thy much-loved master from thy nicer sense.
Dying his lord he owned, viewed him all o'er
With eager eyes, then closed those eyes well
　　pleased.

THE MAD DOG

When Sirius reigns and the sun's parching
　　beams
Bake the dry gaping surface, visit thou
Each ev'n and morn, with quick observant eye
Thy panting pack.　If in dark sullen mood
The glouting hound refuse his wonted meal,
Retiring to some close obscure retreat,
Gloomy disconsolate—with speed remove
The poor infectious wretch, and in strong chains
Bind him, suspected.　Thus that dire disease
Which art can't cure wise caution may prevent.
But, this neglected, soon expect a change,
A dismal change, confusion, frenzy, death.

Or in some dark recess the senseless brute
Sits sadly pining : deep melancholy
And black despair upon his clouded brow
Hang lowering ; from his half-opening jaws
The clammy venom and infectious froth
Distilling fall ; and from his lungs inflamed
Malignant vapours taint the ambient air,
Breathing perdition : his dim eyes are glazed,
He droops his pensive head, his trembling limbs
No more support his weight ; abject he lies,
Dumb, spiritless, benumbed ; till death at last
Gracious attends, and kindly brings relief.

Or, if outrageous grown, behold, alas !
A yet more dreadful scene ; his glaring eyes
Redden with fury, like some angry boar
Churning he foams ; and on his back erect
His pointed bristles rise ; his tail incurved
He drops, and with harsh broken howling rends
The poison-tainted air, with rough hoarse voice
Incessant bays ; and snuffs the infectious breeze ;
This way and that he stares aghast, and starts
At his own shade : jealous, as if he deemed
The world his foes.   If haply towards the stream
He cast his roving eye, cold horror chills
His soul ; averse he flies, trembling, appalled.

DONE TO DEATH

If now perchance through the weak fence
    escaped,
Far up the wind he roves, with open mouth
Inhales the cooling breeze ; nor man nor beast

He spares implacable. . . .
Hence to the village with pernicious haste
Baleful he bends his course : the village flies
Alarmed ; the tender mother in her arms
Hugs close the trembling babe ; the doors are
     barred,
And flying curs by native instinct taught
Shun the contagious bane ; the rustic bands
Hurry to arms, the rude militia seize
Whate'er at hand they find, clubs, forks, or guns ;
From every quarter charge the furious foe
In wild disorder and uncouth array :
Till, now with wounds on wounds oppressed and
     gored,
At one short poisonous gasp he breathes his last.

HYDROPHOBIA

  Sing, philosophic muse, the dire effects
Of this contagious bite on man.
The rustic swains, by long tradition taught
Of leeches old, as soon as they perceive
The bite impressed, to the sea coasts repair.
Plunged in the briny flood, th' unhappy youth
Now journeys home secure ; but soon shall wish
The seas as yet had covered him beneath
The foaming surge.
                    At last with boundless sway
The tyrant frenzy reigns : for as the dog
(Whose fatal bite conveyed th' infectious bane)
Raving he foams, and howls, and barks, and
     bites,

His nature and his actions all canine.
See there distressed he lies, parched up with
    thirst,
But dares not drink.   Till now at last his soul
Trembling escapes.

                Somervile.

LXXIV

BULL-BAITING

A YET ignobler band is guarded round
    With dogs of war—the spurning bull their
        prize ;
And now he bellows, humbled to the ground,
    And now they sprawl in howlings to the skies.

              Lovibond.

LXXV

THE FOX HUNT

TRUEMAN, whom for sagacious nose we hail
The chief, first touched the scarce-distinguished
    gale ;
His tongue was doubtful, and no hound replies :
'Haux !—wind him !—haux !' the tuneful hunts-
    man cries.
At once the list'ning pack asunder spread,
With tail erect, and with inquiring head :
With busy nostrils they foretaste their prey,
And snuff the lawn-impearling dews away.

Now here, now there, they chop upon the scent,
Their tongues in undulating ether spent:
More joyous now, and louder by degrees,
Warm and more warm they catch the coming
    breeze.
Now with full symphony they jointly hail
The welcome tidings of a surer gale;
Along the vale they pour the swelling note,
Their ears and dewlaps on the morning float.
How vainly art aspires by rival sounds
To match the native melody of hounds!
Now lightly o'er opposing walls we bound,
Clear the broad trench, and top the rising mound:
No stop, no time for respite or recess—
On, and still on, fox, dogs, and horses press.

But Reynard, hotly pushed, and close pursued,
Yet fruitful in expedients to elude,
When to the bourn's refreshing bank he came
Had plunged all reeking in the friendly stream.

The chopfall'n hounds meantime are heard no
    more,
But silent range along the winding shore.
Hopeless alike the hunters lag behind,
And give all thoughts of Reynard to the wind,
All, save one wily rival of his art,
Who vows unpitying vengeance ere they part.
Along the coast his watchful course he bent,
Careful to catch and wind the thwarting scent
And last, to make his boastful promise good,
Entered the precincts of the fatal wood.

There through the gloom he leads one hopeless
    train,
And cheers the long-desponding pack in vain ;
Till Ringwood first the faint effluvia caught,
And with loud tongue reformed their old default.

Here had the felon earthed : with many a hound
And many a horse we gird his hold around :
The hounds 'fore Heav'n their accusation spread,
And cry for justice on his caitiff head.

Brooke.

LXXVI

A NEW POINT OF VIEW

BEHOLD the feeble deer, what war they rage ;
In timid breasts what baleful furies rage !
For death reciprocal each forehead bounds ;
In mercy, feeling Cæsar, send the hounds.

Elphinston (MARTIAL).

LXXVII

A ROMAN TRIBUTE

BUT can you waft across the British tide
And land undangered on the further side,
O what great gains will certainly redound
From a free traffic in the British hound.

Mind not the badness of their forms or face—
That the sole blemish of the gen'rous race.
When the bold game turns back upon the spear,
And all the Furies wait upon the war,
First in the fight the whelps of Britain shine,
And snatch, Epirus, all the palm from thine.

Would you chase the deer,
Or urge the motions of the smaller hare,
Let the brisk greyhound of the Celtic name
Bound o'er the glebe and show his painted frame.
Swift as the wing that sails adown the wind,
Swift as the wish that darts along the mind,
The Celtic greyhound sweeps the level lea,
Eyes as he strains and stops the flying prey,
But should the game elude his watchful eyes
No nose sagacious tells him where it lies.

Whitaker (FALISCUS).

LXXVIII

A GREEK COMPLIMENT

A SMALL bold breed, and steady to the game,
Next claims the tribute of peculiar fame,
Trained by the tribes on Britain's wildest shore,
Thence they their title of Agasses bore.
Small as the race that, useless to their lord,
Bask on the hearth, and beg about the board ;

Crook-limbed, and black-eyed, all their frame
    appears
Flanked with no flesh, and bristled rough with
    hairs,
But shod each foot with hardest claws is seen
The sole's kind armour on the beaten green ;
But fenced each jaw with closest teeth around,
And death sits instant on th' inflicted wound.
Far o'er the rest he quests the secret prey,
And sees each track wide opening to his ray :
Far o'er the rest he feels each scent that blows
Court the live nerve, and thrill along the nose.

                Whitaker (OPPIAN).

LXXIX

THE DEEP-TONED JOWLER

ONE hound alone has crossed the dreary height,
The deep-toned Jowler, ever staunch and true.
The chase was o'er . . .
The tents were reared, and fires of evening
    shone.
The mountain's sounds had perished in the
    gloom,
All save the unwearied Jowler's swelling tone,
That bore to trembling stag the sounds of doom,
While every cave of night rolled back the breath-
    ing boom.

The impassioned huntsman wended up the brae,
And loud the order of desistance bawled ;
But ay, as louder waxed his tyrant's say,
Louder and fiercer, Jowler, unappalled,
Across the glen, along the mountain, brawled,
Unpractised he to part till blood was seen :
Though sore by precipice and darkness galled,
He turned his dewlap to the starry sheen,
And howled in furious tone, with yelp and bay
    between.

*   *   *   *

There stood the monarch of the wild at bay
(The impetuous Jowler howling at his brow),
His cheeks all drenched with brine, his antlers
    grey,
Moving across the cliff, majestic, slow,
Like living fairy trees of blenched and leafless
    bough.
With ruthless shaft they pierced his heavy breast,
The baited, thirsty Jowler laps his blood ;
The Royal hunter his brave hound caressed,
Lauded his zeal and spirit unsubdued ;
While the staunch victor, of approval proud,
Rolled his brown back upon the prostrate slain,
Capered around in playful, whelpish mood,
As if unspent by all his toil and pain,
Then licked his crimson flue, and looked to the
    hills again.

                                    Hogg.

LXXX

THE BAFFLED STAGHOUNDS

Yelled on the view the opening pack,
Rock, glen and cavern paid them back ;
To many a mingled sound at once
The awakened mountains gave response.
A hundred dogs bayed deep and strong,
Clattered a hundred steeds along.

— Jaded now, and spent with toil,
Embossed with foam, and dark with soil,
While every gasp with sobs he drew,
The labouring stag strained full in view.
Two dogs of black Saint Hubert's breed,
Unmatched for courage, breath, and speed,
Fast on his flying traces came
And all but won that desperate game ;
For scarce a spear's-length from his haunch
Vindictive toiled the bloodhounds staunch,
Nor nearer might the dogs attain,
Nor farther might the quarry strain.

Close on the hounds the hunter came
To cheer them on the vanished game.

Then through the dell his horn resounds,
From vain pursuit to call the hounds.
Back limped, with slow and crippled pace,
The sulky leaders of the chase ;

Close to their master's side they pressed,
With drooping tail and humbled crest;
But still the dingle's hollow throat
Prolonged the swelling bugle-note.

Scott.

LXXXI

LUFRA AVENGED

THE Monarch saw the gambols flag,
And bade let loose a gallant stag,
Whose pride the holiday to crown,
Two favourite greyhounds should pull down,
That venison free, and Bordeaux wine,
Might serve the archery to dine.
But Lufra,—whom from Douglas' side
Nor bribe nor threat could e'er divide,
The fleetest hound in all the north,—
Brave Lufra saw, and darted forth.
She left the royal hounds midway,
And dashing on the antlered prey,
Sunk her sharp muzzle in his flank,
And deep the flowing life-blood drank.
The King's stout huntsman saw the sport
By strange intruder broken short,
Came up, and with his leash unbound
In anger struck the noble hound.
    The Douglas had endured that morn,
The King's cold look, the nobles' scorn,

And last, and worst to spirit proud,
Had borne the pity of the crowd ;
But Lufra had been fondly bred,
To share his board, to watch his bed,
And oft would Ellen Lufra's neck
In maiden glee with garlands deck ;
They were such playmates, that with name
Of Lufra, Ellen's image came.
His stifled wrath is brimming high
In darkened brow and flashing eye :
As waves before the bark divide
The crowd gave way before his stride ;
Needs but a buffet and no more,
The groom lies senseless in his gore.

Scott.

LXXXII

THE HEÄRE

(DREE O'M PEASANTS A-TA'KEN O'T)

First.— There be the greyhounds ! lok ! an'
there's the heäre !

Second.—What houn's, the squier's, Thomas ?
where, then, where ?

First.— Why, out in Ash Hill, near the barn,
behine thik tree.

Third.— The pollard ?

First.— Pollard ! no, b' ye bline ?

Second.—There, I do zee em awver-right thik cow.

Third.— The red oone ?

First.— No, a mile beyand her now.

Third.— Oh ! there's the heäre, a-meäkèn for the
drong.

Second.—My goodness ! How the dogs do zweep
along,

A-pokèn out their pweinted noses' tips.

Third.— 'E can't allow hizzuf much time vor
slips !

First.— They'll hab'en, a'ter all, I'll bet a crown.

Second.—Done vor a crown. They woon't ! 'E's
gwäin to groun' ;

Third.— He is !

First.— He idden !

Third.— Ah ! 'tis well his tooes
Ha' got noo corns, inside o' hobnäil
shoes.

First.— He's geäme a-runnèn too. Why, he do
mwore
Than eärn his life.

Third.— His life wer' his avore.

First.— There, now the dogs wull turn en.

Second.—No ! He's right.

First.— He idden !

Second.—Ees he is !

Third.— He's out o' zight.

First.— Aye, aye. His mettle wull be well
a-tried
Agwäin down Verny Hill, o' t'other zide.
They 'll have en there.

Third.— Oh ! no, a vew good hops
    Wull teäke en on to Knapton Lower
    copse.

Second.—An' that's a meesh that he 've a-took
    avore.

Third.— Ees, that's his hwome.

First.— He 'll never reach his door.

Second.—He wull.

First.— He woon't.

Third.— Now, hark, d'ye heär em now ?

Second.—Oh ! here's a bwoy a-come athirt the
    brow
    O' Knapton Hill. We 'll ax en.

First.— Here, my bwoy !
    Canst tell us where's the heäre ?

Boy.— He 's got awoy.

Second.—Ees, got awoy, in coo'se, I never zeed
    A heäre a-scotèn on wi' haef his
    speed.

First.— Why, there, the dogs be wold, and haef
    a-done.
    They can't catch anything wi' lags to
    run.

Second.—Vrom vu'st to laste they had but little
    chance
    O' catchen o'n.

Third.— They had a perty dance.

First.— No ! catch en, no ! I little thought they
    would ;
    He know'd his road too well to Knapton
    Wood.

Third.— No! no! I wish the squier would let
      me feäre
        On rabbits till his hounds do catch thik
        heäre.

Barnes.

LXXXIII

FINN AND OSSIAN HUNTING

Fin and Oshin went out to hunt,
Fal lal loo as fal lal la !
With a noble train of men and dogs,
Not less in number than a hundred men,
So swift of foot and keen, none were their like ;
With scores of bandogs fierce they sallied forth
O'er hill and dale much havoc for to make.
Whom left they at home but youthful Orree !
Who slept secure beneath the shadowy rock.
Full threescore greyhounds with their whelps
      they left,
As many old dames to attend the young.

Unknown.

PART III

ELEGIAC POEMS

Should Adamantius, my dog, be laid along,
Downe in some ditch without his exequies,
Or epitaphs, or mournful elegies?

JOSEPH HALL.

MELAMPUS' EPITAPH

ALL that a dog could have
The good Melampus had:
Nay, he had more than what in beasts we
    crave,
For he could play the brave,
And often, like a Thraso stern, go mad:
And if ye had not seen, but heard him bark,
Ye would have sworn he was your parish clerk.

Drummond.

UPON HIS SPANIEL TRACIE.

Now thou art dead, no eye shall ever see
For shape and service spaniel like to thee.
This shall my love do, give thy sad death one
Tear, that deserves of me a million.

Herrick.

SHOCK AND HIS MISTRESS

Shock's fate I mourn; poor Shock is now no
    more!
Ye Muses mourn: ye chambermaids deplore.
Unhappy Shock! yet more unhappy fair,
Doomed to survive thy joy and only care!
Thy wretched fingers now no more shall deck,
And tie the favourite riband round his neck;
No more thy hand shall smooth his glossy hair,
And comb the wavings of his pendent ear.
Yet cease thy flowing grief, forsaken maid!
All mortal pleasures in a moment fade;
Our surest hope is in an hour destroyed;
And love, best gift of Heav'n, not long enjoyed.

Methinks I see her frantic with despair,
Her streaming eyes, wrung hands, and flowing
    hair;
Her Mechlin pinners, rent, the floor bestrow,
And her torn fan gives signs of real woe.
Hence superstition, that tormenting guest,
That haunts with fancied fears the coward breast,
No dread events upon this fate attend,
Stream eyes no more, no more thy tresses rend.
Though certain omens oft forewarn a state,
And dying lions show the monarch's fate;
Why should such fears bid Celia's sorrow rise?
For, when a Lap-dog falls, no lover dies.

Cease, Celia, cease; restrain thy flowing tears;
Some warmer passion will dispel thy cares.
In man you 'll find a more substantial bliss,
More grateful toying, and a sweeter kiss.
   He 's dead.   Oh, lay him gently in the ground!
And may his tomb be by this verse renowned:
'Here Shock, the pride of all his kind, is laid,
Who fawned like man, but ne'er like man be-
    trayed.'

Gay.

LXXXVII

A PROUD BOAST

I NEVER barked when out of season;
I never bit without a reason;
I ne'er insulted weaker brother;
Nor wronged by force or fraud another.
Though brutes are placed a rank below,
Happy for man could he say so!

Blacklock.

LXXXVIII

THE TRUSTY LYDIA

THE amphitheatre, my scene;
A huntress, by the masters bred:
At home, ingenuous, fond, serene;
Tho' of the forests fierce the dread.

The trusty Lydia was my name :
My faith so by my patron prized,
To me, he spurned each dog of fame ;
And had Erigone's despised :

Had flouted him, renowned of old,
For true sublime Dictian breed ;
Who solaced Cephalus, we 're told ;
Alike, among the stars, decreed.

Not wasteful time, or useless age,
That laid the staunch Dulichian low,
Have swept fair Lydia from the stage ;
Or fang of any common foe.

But, by the lightning of a boar,
Tremendous, Calydon, as thine ;
O Erymanthus, was I tore ;
His equal, who had torn thy pine.

Nor can I then, tho' bold, complain,
That to the shades, so rapt, I fly,
No matchless merit could obtain,
A more exalted death to die.

Elphinston (Martial).

LXXXIX

A RIDDLE

Here lies one who never drew
Blood himself, yet many slew ;
Gave the gun its aim, and figure
Made in field, yet ne'er pulled trigger ;

Armèd men have gladly made
Him their guide, and him obeyed ;
At his signified desire,
Would advance, present, and fire—
Stout he was, and large of limb,
Scores have fled in spite of him :
And to all this fame he rose,
Only following his nose.
Neptune was he called ; not he
Who controls the boist'rous sea,
But of happier command,
Neptune of the furrowed land ;
And, your wonder vain to shorten,
Pointer to Sir John Throckmorton.

Cowper.

xc

FOP

THOUGH once a puppy, and though Fop by name,
Here moulders one whose bones some honour
claim.
No sycophant, although of spaniel race,
And, though no hound, a martyr to the chase—
Ye squirrels, rabbits, leverets, rejoice,
Your haunts no longer echo to his voice ;
This record of his fate exulting view,
He died worn out with vain pursuit of you.

' Yes '—the indignant shade of Fop replies—
' And worn with vain pursuit man also dies.'

Cowper.

XCI

EPITAPH ON A SPANIEL

HERE rest the relics of a friend below,
Blest with more sense than half the folks I know;
Fond of his ease and to no parties prone,
He damned no sect, but calmly gnawed his bone;
Performed his functions well in every way,—
Blush, Christians, if you can, and copy Tray.

Peter Pindar (*Wolcot*).

XCII

DESERTED DIED

APPROACH, vain man! and bid thy pride be mute;
Start not—this monument records a brute;
In sculptured shrine may sleep some human hog—
This stone is sacred to a faithful dog.
Though reason lend her boastful ray to thee,
From faults which make it useless he was free:
He broke no oath, betrayed no trusting friend,
Nor ever fawned for an unworthy end;
His life was shortened by no slothful ease,
Vice-begot care, or folly-bred disease.
Forsook by him he valued more than life,
His generous nature sank beneath the strife;

Left by his master on a foreign shore,
New masters offered—but he would no more ;
The ocean oft with seeming sorrow eyed,
And pierced by man's ingratitude he died.

Erskine.

XCII

SILENT ECHO

In wood and wild, ye warbling throng,
　　Your heavy loss deplore ;
Now, half extinct your powers of song,
　　Sweet ' Echo ' is no more.

Ye jarring, screeching things around,
　　Scream your discordant joys ;
Now, half your din of tuneless sound
　　With ' Echo ' silent lies.

Burns.

XCIV

SHIPWRECKED TIPPOO

Here, stranger, pause, nor view with scornful eyes
The stone which marks where faithful Tippoo lies :
Freely kind nature gave each liberal grace,
Which most ennobles and exalts our race :
Excelling strength and beauty joined in me,
Ingenuous worth, and firm fidelity.

Nor shame I to have borne a tyrant's name,
So far unlike to his my spotless fame.
Cast by a fatal storm on Tenby's coast,
Reckless of life, I wailed my master lost,
Whom, long contending with the o'erwhelming
    wave,
In vain with fruitless love I strove to save.
I, only I, alas! surviving, bore
His dying trust, his tablets, to the shore.
Kind welcome from the Belgian race I found,
Who, once in times remote, to British ground
Strangers like me came from a foreign strand.
I loved at large along the extended sand
To roam, and oft beneath the swelling wave,
Though known so fatal once, my limbs to lave;
Or join the children in their summer play,
First in their sports, companion of their way.
Thus while from many a hand a meal I sought,
Winter and age had certain misery brought;
But fortune smiled, a safe and blessed abode
A new-found master's generous love bestowed,
And, 'midst these shades, where smiling flow'rets
    bloom,
Gave me a happy life and honoured tomb.

Grenville.

XCV

TROUNCER, THE FOXES' FOE

Poor faithful Trouncer! thou canst lead no more;
All thy fatigues and all thy triumphs o'er!

Triumphs of worth, whose long excelling fame
Was still to follow true the hunted game !
Beneath enormous oaks, Britannia's boast,
In thick, impenetrable coverts lost,
When the warm pack in falt'ring silence stood,
Thine was the note that roused the list'ning wood,
Rekindling every joy with tenfold force,
Through all the mazes of the tainted course.
Still foremost thou the dashing stream to cross,
And tempt along the animated horse ;
Foremost o'er fen or level mead to pass,
And sweep the show'ring dew-drops from the
    grass ;
Then bright emerging from the mist below
To climb the woodland hill's exulting brow.
Pride of thy race ! with worth far less than thine,
Full many human leaders daily shine !
Less faith, less constancy, less gen'rous zeal !—
Then no disgrace my humble verse shall feel,
Where not one lying line to riches bows,
Or poisoned sentiments from rancour flows ;
Nor flowers are strewn around Ambition's car :
An honest dog 's a nobler theme by far.
Each sportsman heard the tidings with a sigh,
When death's cold touch had stopped his tune-
    ful cry ;
And though high deeds, and fair exalted praise,
In memory lived, and flowed in rustic lays,
Short was the strain of monumental woe :
' Foxes, rejoice ! here buried lies your foe.'

                    Bloomfield.

IN MEMORY OF MUSIC

LIE here, without a record of thy worth,
Beneath a covering of the common earth!
It is not from unwillingness to praise,
Or want of love, that here no stone we raise;
More thou deserv'st; but *this* man gives to man,
Brother to brother; *this* is all we can.
Yet they to whom thy virtues made thee dear
Shall find thee through all changes of the year:
This Oak points out thy grave; the silent tree
Will gladly stand a monument of thee.

We grieved for thee, and wished thy end were past;
And willingly have laid thee here at last:
For thou hadst lived till everything that cheers
In thee had yielded to the weight of years;
Extreme old age had wasted thee away,
And left thee but a glimmering of the day;
Thy ears were deaf, and feeble were thy knees,—
I saw thee stagger in the summer breeze,
Too weak to stand against its sportive breath,
And ready for the gentlest stroke of death.

It came, and we were glad; yet tears were shed;
Both man and woman wept when thou wert dead;
Not only for a thousand thoughts that were,
Old household thoughts, in which thou hadst thy
        share;

But for some precious boons vouchsafed to thee,
Found scarcely anywhere in like degree !
For love, that comes wherever life and sense
Are given by God, in thee was most intense ;
A chain of heart, a feeling of the mind,
A tender sympathy, which did thee bind,
Not only to us Men, but to thy Kind :
Yea, for thy fellow-brutes in thee we saw
A soul of love, love's intellectual law :—
Hence, if we wept, it was not done in shame ;
Our tears from passion and from reason came,
And, therefore, shalt thou be an honoured name.

Wordsworth.

XCVII

MAIDA

BENEATH the sculptured form which late you
    wore,
Sleep soundly, Maida, at your master's door.

Scott.

XCVIII

EXEMPLARY NICK

HERE lies poor Nick, an honest creature,
Of faithful, gentle, courteous nature ;
A parlour pet unspoiled by favour,
A pattern of good dog behaviour.

Without a wish, without a dream,
Beyond his home and friends at Cheam,
Contentedly through life he trotted
Along the path that fate allotted ;
Till Time, his aged body wearing,
Bereaved him of his sight and hearing,
Then laid him down without a pain
To sleep, and never wake again.

Sydney Smith.

XCIX

CANINE IMMORTALITY

AND they have drowned thee then at last ! poor
    Phillis !
The burden of old age was heavy on thee,
And yet thou shouldst have lived !   What
    though thine eye
Was dim, and watched no more with eager joy
The wonted call that on thy dull sense sunk
With fruitless repetition, the warm sun
Might still have cheered thy slumber : thou
    didst love
To lick the hand that fed thee, and though past
Youth's active season, even life itself
Was comfort.   Poor old friend ! how earnestly
Would I have pleaded for thee ! thou hadst been
Still the companion of my childish sports :

And as I roamed o'er Avon's woody cliffs,
From many a day-dream has thy short quick
    bark
Recalled my wandering soul.   I have beguiled
Often the melancholy hours at school,
Soured by some little tyrant, with the thought
Of distant home, and I remembered then
Thy faithful fondness: for not mean the joy,
Returning at the pleasant holidays,
I felt from thy dumb welcome.   Pensively
Sometimes have I remarked thy slow decay,
Feeling myself changed too, and musing much
On many a sad vicissitude of life !
Ah, poor companion! when thou followedst
    last
Thy master's parting footsteps to the gate
Which closed for ever on him, thou didst lose
Thy truest friend, and none was left to plead
For the old age of brute fidelity !
But fare thee well !   Mine is no narrow creed ;
And He who gave thee being did not frame
The mystery of life to be the sport
Of merciless man !   There is another world
For all that live and move—a better one !
Where the proud bipeds, who would fain con-
    fine
Infinite goodness to the little bounds
Of their own charity, may envy thee !

                                    Robert Southey.

c

BLIND IRUS' WOLF-DOG

Poor Irus' faithful wolf-dog, here I lie,
That wont to tend my old blind master's steps,
His guide and guard; nor, while my service
    lasted,
Had he occasion for that staff, with which
He now goes picking out his path in fear
Over the highways and crossings; but would plant,
Safe in the conduct of my friendly string,
A firm foot forward still, till he had reached
His poor seat on some stone, nigh where the tide
Of passers-by in thickest confluence flowed:
To whom with loud and passionate laments
From morn to eve his dark estate he wailed;
Nor wailed to all in vain: some here and there,
The well-disposed and good, their pennies gave.
I meantime at his feet obsequious slept;
Not all asleep in sleep, but heart and ear
Pricked up at his least motion; to receive
At his kind hand my customary crumbs
And common portion in his feast of scraps;
Or when night warned us homeward, tired and
    spent
With our long day and tedious beggary.
These were my manners, this my way of life,
Till age and slow disease me overtook,
And severed from my sightless master's side.

But lest the grace of so good deeds should die,
Through tract of years in mute oblivion lost,
This slender tomb of turf hath Irus reared,
Cheap monument of no ungrudging hand,
And with short verse inscribed it, to attest,
In long and lasting union to attest,
The virtues of the beggar and his dog.

Lamb.

CI

POOR DOG TRAY

On the green banks of Shannon, when Sheelah
    was nigh,
No blithe Irish lad was so happy as I ;
No harp like my own could so cheerily play,
And wherever I went was my poor dog Tray.

When at last I was forced from my Sheelah to
    part,
She said (while the sorrow was big at her heart):
' Oh ! remember your Sheelah when far, far
    away,
And be kind, my dear Pat, to our poor dog Tray.'

Poor dog ! he was faithful and kind, to be sure,
And he constantly loved me, although I was
    poor ;
When the sour-looking folks sent me heartless
    away,
I had always a friend in my poor dog Tray.

When the road was so dark, and the night was
    so cold,
And Pat and his dog were grown weary and old,
How snugly we slept in my old coat of grey,
And he licked me for kindness—my poor dog Tray.

Though my wallet was scant, I remembered his
    case,
Nor refused my last crust to his pitiful face ;
But he died at my feet on a cold winter's day,
And I played a lament for my poor dog Tray.

Where now shall I go, poor, forsaken, and blind?
Can I find one to guide me, so faithful and kind ?
To my sweet native village, so far, far away,
I can ne'er more return with my poor dog Tray.

                  Campbell.

CII

MANX

AND is all sense, all feeling gone,
    All sign of latent life ;
The panting breast, the feeble moan,
    The gentle spirit's strife,
When love with weakness struggled sore
To lick his mistress' hand once more ?
Yes ! all is o'er ; poor Manx is dead,
    And the infrequent tear
From eyes not prone to weep is shed
    On Manx's humble bier ;

O'er him, the faithful, fond, and mild,
Though long beloved, by love unspoiled.
Yet not untimely was his death,
    For age had blanched his hair;
And his weak form and quivering breath
    Were kept alive by care;
Such care as rears the new-fall'n lamb
When biting frosts have killed its dam.

And well had he such care deserved,
    When age and sickness fell,
From her who in his youth he served
    So faithfully and well.
From life's first cry to death's last moan
No other mistress had he known;
And though so weak his trembling frame,
Yet still his step to meet me came,
    His eye was turned on me;
And more I loved as more I feared,
And every care the more endeared.

Witness of Friendship's social talk,
    Of sweet affection's praise,
Linked in with every pleasant thought,
That hope inspired or memory taught.
Oh, few and mournful flowers have stood
    November's blast and dew,
Yet one last rose, sad southernwood,
    Pale lavender and rue,
Myrtle and cistus' balmy breath
Shall sweeten thy dear corse in death!

Oh, harsh and broken is the lyre
 And all untuned the string,
And yet, though quenched the minstrel fire,
 Still, still of Manx I sing;
And long the rude lament shall swell
For him who loved and served so well.
     Mary Russell Mitford.

CIII

FLEET MARMION

FAREWELL! a long farewell to thee,
 The fleetest, bravest hound
That ever coursed on hill or lea,
 Or swept the heathy ground;
Foremost, whatever dog was there,
My Marmion! slayer of the hare!

Farewell! a long farewell to thee,
 The fondest, dearest, best,
That ever played around my knee,
 Or leaped upon my breast;
By all beloved, and loving all,
My Marmion! favourite of the hall!

Thou diedst when Fame's bright wreath was
  nearest
 On Ilsley's dreary heath;
I should have sung thy triumph, dearest,
 And not have mourned thy death;

Most cherished in that parting hour
Which showed thy love's undying power!

Who dreamed of death that gazed on thee?
    Thy light and golden form,
Skimming along the meadowy sea,
    A sunbeam in the storm!
From air and fire derived, thy birth
Had nought to do with drossy earth!

With spirit dancing in thine eye,
    Love brooding in thy breast,
Gay as the flower-fed butterfly,
    Calm as the turtle's nest;
Free from the care, the thought of man,
Bliss crowned thy being's little span.

And loved in life, and mourned in death,
    Upon thy simple bier
The rose and myrtle's fragrant breath
    Blend with affection's tear;
And proudly verdant laurels wave
Their branches o'er my Marmion's grave.

And long thy memory shall live,
    And long thy well-earned fame,
And oft a sigh shall coursers give
    At thy remembered name;
And long thy mistress' heart shall tell
The sadness of her last farewell!

Mary Russell Mitford.

CIV

THE CYNOTAPH

Poor Tray Charmant!
Poor Tray de mon ami!
DOG-BURY AND VERGERS.

OH! where shall I bury my poor dog Tray,
Now his fleeting breath has passed away?
Seventeen years, I can venture to say,
Have I seen him gambol, and frolic, and play,
Ever more happy, and frisky, and gay,
As though every one of his months was May,
And the whole of his life one long holiday—
Now he's a lifeless lump of clay,
Oh! where shall I bury my faithful Tray?

I am almost tempted to think it hard
That it may not be there, in yon sunny church-
    yard
            Where the green willows wave
            O'er the peaceful grave,
Which holds all that once was honest and brave,
Kind and courteous, and faithful, and true;
Qualities, Tray, that were found in you.
But it may not be—yon sacred ground,
By holiest feelings fenced around,
May ne'er within its hallowed bound
Receive the dust of a soulless hound.

I would not place him in yonder fane,
Where the mid-day sun through the storied pane
Throws on the pavement a crimson stain;

    *   *   *   *

No!—Tray's humble tomb would look but shabby
'Mid the sculptured shrines of that gorgeous
    Abbey.
        Besides, in the place
        They say there's not space
To bury what wet-nurses call 'a Babby.'
Even 'Rare Ben Jonson,' that famous wight,
I am told, is interred there bolt upright,
In just such a posture, beneath his bust,
As Tray used to sit in to beg for a crust.
        The epitaph, too,
        Would scarcely do:
For what could it say but 'Here lies Tray,
A very good dog of a kind in his day'?

I would not place him beneath thy walls,
And proud o'ershadowing dome, St. Paul's!

    *   *   *   *

        No, Tray, we must yield,
        And go further a-field;
To lay you by Nelson were downright effront'ry;
—We'll be off from the city, and look at the
    country.

        It shall not be there,
        In that sepulchred square,
Where folks are interred for the sake of the air.

(Though, pay but the dues, they could hardly
    refuse
To Tray what they grant to Thugs and Hindoos,
Turks, Infidels, Heretics, Jumpers and Jews.)

      *   *   *   *

      Nor shall he be laid
      By that cross Old Maid,
Miss Penelope Bird,—of whom it is said
All the dogs in the parish were ever afraid.

      No,—if Tray were interred
      By Penelope Bird,
No dog would be e'er so be-'whelp'ed and be-
    'cur'red—
All the night long her cantankerous Sprite
Would be running about in the pale moonlight,
Chasing him round, and attempting to lick
The ghost of poor Tray with the ghost of a stick.

    Stay!—let me see!—Ay—here it shall be,
At the root of the gnarled and time-worn tree,
      Where Tray and I
      Would often lie,
And watch the bright clouds as they floated by
In the broad expanse of the clear blue sky,
When the sun was bidding the world good-bye;
And the plaintive nightingale, warbling nigh,
Poured forth her mournful melody;
While the tender wood-pigeon's cooing cry
Has made me say to myself, with a sigh,
'How nice you would eat with a steak in a pie!'

Ay, here it shall be! far, far from the view
Of the noisy world and its maddening crew.
   Simple and few,
   Tender and true
The lines o'er his grave.—They have, some of
  them, too,
The advantage of being remarkably new.

EPITAPH

   Affliction sore
   Long time he bore,
Physicians were in vain!
   Grown blind, alas! he'd
   Some prussic acid,
And that put him out of his pain!

Barham.

CV

BOATSWAIN, HIS ONE FRIEND

WHEN some proud son of man returns to earth,
Unknown to glory, but upheld by birth,
The sculptor's art exhausts the pomp of woe,
And storied urns record who rests below;
When all is done, upon the tomb is seen,
Not what he was, but what he should have been:
But the poor dog, in life the firmest friend,
The first to welcome, foremost to defend,

Whose honest heart is still his master's own,
Who labours, fights, lives, breathes for him alone,
Unhonoured falls, unnoticed all his worth,
Denied in heaven the soul he held on earth :
While man, vain insect ! hopes to be forgiven,
And claims himself a sole, exclusive heaven.
O man ! thou feeble tenant of an hour,
Debased by slavery, or corrupt by power,
Who knows thee well must quit thee with disgust,
Degraded mass of animated dust !
Thy love is lust, thy friendship all a cheat,
Thy smiles hypocrisy, thy words deceit !
By nature vile, ennobled but by name,
Each kindred brute might bid thee blush for
　　shame.
Ye ! who, perchance, behold this simple urn,
Pass on—it honours none you wish to mourn :
To mark a friend's remains these stones arise ;
I never knew but one, and here he lies.

Byron.

CVI

LOUIS

No cold philosophy nor cynic sneer
Checks the unbidden and the honest tear ;
What little difference and how short the span
Betwixt thy instinct and the mind of man !

Fitzhardinge.

CVII

THE DROWNED SPANIEL

THE day-long bluster of the storm was o'er,
The sands were bright; the winds had fallen
   asleep,
And, from the far horizon, o'er the deep
   The sunset swam unshadowed to the shore.

High up, the rainbow had not passed away,
When, roving o'er the shingle beach, I found
A little waif, a spaniel newly drowned;
   The shining waters kissed him as he lay.

In some kind heart thy gentle memory dwells,
I said, and, though thy latest aspect tells
   Of drowning pains and mortal agony,
   Thy master's self might weep and smile to see
His little dog stretched on these rosy shells,
   Betwixt the rainbow and the rosy sea.

Tennyson Turner.

CVIII

ON AN IRISH RETRIEVER

TEN years of loving loyalty
   Unthankèd should not go to earth,
And I, who had no less from thee,
   Devote this tribute to thy worth.

For thou didst give to me, old friend,
　　Thy service while thy life did last;
Thy life and service have an end,
　　And here I thank thee for the past.

Trusted and faithful, tried and true,
　　Watchful and swift to do my will,
Grateful for care that was thy due,
　　To duty's call obedient still.

From ill thou knew'st thou didst refrain,
　　The good thou knew'st thou strove to do,
Nor dream of fame, nor greed of gain,
　　Man's keenest spurs, urged thee thereto.

Brute, with a heart of human love,
　　And speechless soul of instinct fine!
How few by reason's law who move
　　Deserve an epitaph like thine!

Fanny Kemble (*Butler*).

CIX

A SPARK DIVINE

Not hopeless, round this calm sepulchral spot,
　　A wreath presaging life we twine;
If God be love, what sleeps below was not
　　Without a spark divine.

Doyle.

cx

KAISER DEAD

What, Kaiser dead? The heavy news
Post-haste to Cobham calls the Muse,
From where in Farringford she brews
        The ode sublime,
Or with Pen-bryn's bold bard pursues
        A rival rhyme.

Kai's bracelet tail, Kai's busy feet,
Were known to all the village street.
'What, poor Kai dead?' say all I meet;
        'A loss indeed!'
O for the croon pathetic, sweet,
        Of Robin's reed!

Six years ago I brought him down,
A baby dog, from London town;
Round his small throat of black and brown
        A ribbon blue,
And vouched by glorious renown
        A dachshound true.

His mother, most majestic dame,
Of blood unmixed, from Potsdam came;
And Kaiser's race we deemed the same—
        No lineage higher.
And so he bore the imperial name.
        But ah, his sire!

Soon, soon the days conviction bring.
The collie hair, the collie swing,
The tail's indomitable ring,
          The eye's unrest—
The case was clear ; a mongrel thing
          Kai stood confest.

But all those virtues, which commend
The humbler sort who serve and tend,
Were thine in store, thou faithful friend.
          What sense, what cheer !
To us, declining tow'rds our end,
          A mate how dear !

          *   *   *   *

Thine eye was bright, thy coat it shone ;
Thou hadst thine errands, off and on ;
In joy thy last morn flew ; anon,
          A fit !   All's over ;
And thou art gone where Geist hath gone,
          And Toss, and Rover.

                              Matthew Arnold.

CXI

TORY, A PUPPY

HE lies in the soft earth under the grass,
Where they who love him often pass.
And his grave is under a tall young lime,
In whose boughs the pale green hop-flowers climb ;
But his spirit—where does his spirit rest ?
It was God who made him—God knows best.

                              Mortimer Collins.

CXII

ISLET THE DACHS

Our Islet out of Helgoland, dismissed
From his quaint tenement, quits hates and loves.
There lived with us a wagging humourist
In that hound's arch dwarf-legged on boxing-
    gloves.

George Meredith.

CXIII

OUR DOG JOCK

A rollicksome frolicsome rare old cock
As ever did nothing was our dog Jock ;
A gleesome, fleasome, affectionate beast,
As slow at a fight, as swift at a feast ;
A wit among dogs, when his life 'gan fail,
One couldn't but see the old wag in his tale,
When his years grew long and his eyes grew dim,
And his course of bark could not strengthen him.
Never more now shall our knees be pressed
By his dear old chops in their slobbery rest,
Nor our mirth be stirred at his solemn looks,
As wise, and as dull, as divinity books.
Our old friend's dead, but we all well know
He's gone to the Kennels where the good dogs go,
Where the cooks be not, but the beef-bones be,
And his old head never need turn for a flea.

Payn.

A LOST FRIEND

Thou little friend who, in my heart
  As in my home, didst find thy rest,
  By all admired, by all caressed,
Must thou and I for ever part?

Now thou art gone, I think of thee,
  As I have seen thee many a day,
  Frisking in merry-hearted play,
Or sleeping, trustful, on my knee.

Oft have I seen thy slumbering face
  Alert with fancied joy or pain!
  Imagination held thy brain
Intent on pleasures of the chase.

How grieved wast thou, forbade to come
  To share my walk, yet patient still!
  How soon subdued thine ardent will!
How prompt to bid me welcome home!

And when thy time was come to die,
  Then didst thou seek the room most dear,
  And breathe thy last all gently there
Where on my lap thou oft didst lie.

Faithful and loving e'er wast thou,
  And faith and love are virtues rare.
  How hard to think that, in the air,
These are for ever vanished now!

Dull souls were they who saw ' no soul'
  In thy quick glance and speaking eye :
  Shall I not meet thee by-and-bye
Thou part of an Eternal Whole ?

Sleep, little form, beneath the ground !
  All that was THOU can not be there.
  Perchance in some far happier sphere
Thy loving soul may yet be found !

Leonard.

CXV

QUESTIONS

WHERE are you now, little wandering
Life, that so faithfully dwelt with us,
Played with us, fed with us, felt with us,
  Years we grew fonder and fonder in?

You who but yesterday sprang to us,
Are we for ever bereft of you ?
And is this all that is left of you—
  One little grave, and a pang to us?

Mallock.

CXVI

OLD ROCKET

WE were sitting in the gun-room, and the long-
  persistent snow
Formed, of course, the leading subject of the chat.
There we smoked and dreamed of hunting when
  the weary frost should go,
  And old Rocket lay extended on the mat.

Poor old Rocket! Gordon setter of the good
　　old-fashioned strain ;
　　Better dog one wouldn't wish for in his
　　　way ;
But his legs were getting shaky, and his nose
　　was on the wane,
　　And he couldn't stand a long and trying day.

There he lay upon the hearth-rug; did he
　　dream of triumphs past,
　　On the mountains 'mid the heather growing
　　　deep ?
Was he ranging some dream-moorland, that his
　　breath should come so fast,
　　And his limbs should strain and quiver in his
　　　sleep ?

He rose, and tried to shake himself, and then
　　he came to me.
　　I patted him: 'Get up, old man, come
　　　on !'
He raised his fore-paws stiffly, his head drooped
　　on my knee,
　　And then I saw the poor old dog had gone.

He'd been a good 'un in his time—no better—
　　so they said,
　　Especially on 'cock and wary snipe ;
And soon they took their candles, said 'Good-
　　night,' and went to bed :
　　His master sat alone, and lit a pipe.

No more, no more?   Ah! never more he 'll sniff
    the mountain air
  In August, when the leaves are lying sere;
Never more his form will stiffen till I hear his
    sculptured prayer:
    'Come along, old friend, I've found 'em—
    they are here!'

The merry Twelfth will come again; the guns
    may rattle fast;
  The birds may spring as blithely as of yore;
But the brightest days will differ from the
    brightness of the past,
  For a true old friend will share them nevermore.

Is a man a hopeless heathen if he dreams of one
    fair day
    When, with spirit free from shadows grey and
    cold,
He may wander through the heather in the
    'unknown far away,'
    With his good old dog before him as of old?

                          Horsfield.

CXVII

LORD ORRERY'S HECTOR

Stranger, behold the mighty Hector's tomb!
See to what end both dogs and Heroes come!
These are the honours by his Master paid
To Hector's Manes and lamented shade.

Nor Words nor Honours can enough commend
The social dog—nay, more—the Faithful Friend.
From Nature all his principles he drew:
By nature faithful, vigilant, and true.
His looks and voice his inward thoughts ex-
　　pressed,
He growled in anger, and in love caressed.
No human falsehood lurked beneath his heart:
Brave without boasting, gen'rous without art.
When Hector's virtues Man, proud Man! displays,
Truth shall adorn his tomb with Hector's praise.

Unknown.

CXVIII

THE GREYHOUND SNOWBALL

HE, who outbounded time and space,
The fleetest of the greyhound race,
Lies here! At length subdued by death,
His speed now stopped, and out of breath.

Ah! gallant Snowball! what remains
Up Fordan's banks, o'er Flixton's plains,
Of all thy strength—thy sinewy force,
Which rather flew than ran the course?

Ah! what remains? save that thy breed
May to their father's fame succeed;
And when the prize appears in view,
May prove that they are Snowballs too.

Unknown.

DOG LATIN

EHEU! hic jacet Crony,
A dog of much renown,
Nec fur, nec macaroni,
Though born and bred in town.

In war he was acerrimus,
In dog-like arts perite,
In love, alas! miserrimus,
For he died of a rival's bite.

His mistress struxit cenotaph;
And, as the verse comes pat in,
Ego qui scribo epitaph
Indite it in dog Latin.

Unknown.

ON SOME ELEGIES ON A LAP-DOG

POOR dog, whom rival poets strive
To celebrate in plaintive strains;
If thou hadst howled so when alive,
Thou hadst been beaten for thy pains.

Unknown.

PART IV

MISCELLANEOUS POEMS

With eye upraised his master's look to scan,
The joy, the solace, and the aid of man;
The rich man's guardian and the poor man's friend,
The only creature faithful to the end.

UNKNOWN.

THE PITIFUL PRIORESS

THERE was also a nun, a prioress . . .
She was so charitable and so piteous
She would weep if that she saw a mouse
Caught in a trap, if it were dead or bled.
Of small hounds had she, that she fed
With roasted flesh, and milk, and wastel-bread,
But sore wept she if one of them were dead,
Or if men smote it with a yard smart
And all was conscience and tender heart.

Chaucer.

BAGSCHE'S COMPLAINT

ALAS! whom to should I complain
    In my extreme necessitie;
Or whom to shall I make my moan?
    In Court na dog will do for me,
    Beseeching some for charitie
To bear my supplication
    To Scudlar, Luffra and Bawtie
Now, ere the King pass from the town.

I have followit the court so lang,
  While, in gude faith I may na mair ;
The country knows I may nocht gang,
  I am so crookèd, auld and sair,
  That I wit not where to repair ;
For, when I had authoritie,
  I thocht me so familiar,
I never dread necessitie.

I rue the race that Geordie Steill
  Brocht Bawtie to the Kingis presence,
I pray God, let him ne'er do weill,
  Since soon I gat na audience ;
  For, Bawtie now gettis sic credence,
That he lies on the Kingis nicht-gown,
  Where I perforce for my offence,
Must, in the close, lie like ane loon.

For I have been, ay to this hour,
  Ane worrier of lamb and hog,
Ane tyrant and ane tulzeour,
  Ane murderer of many ane dog :
  Five foals I chased out thro' ane scrog,
Wherefore their mothers did me warrie ;
  For they were drownit all in ane bog ;
Speir at John Gordon of Pittarie,

Whilk in his house did bring me up,
  And usit me to slay the deer,
Sweet milk and meal he gart me sup,
  That craft I learnit soon perqueir,
  All other virtue ran arrear,

When I began to bark and fight ;
    For there was neither monk, nor friar,
Nor wife, nor bairn, but I wald bite.

When to the King the case was known
    Of my unhappy hardiness,
And all the truth unto him shown,
    How every dog I did oppress ;
    Then, 'gan his grace express,
I should be brocht to his presence ;
    Nochtwithstanding my wickedness,
In court I gat great audience.

     *   *   *   *

So they that gave me to the King,
    I was their mortal enemie,
I took care of no kind of thing,
    But please the Kingis majestie ;
    But when he knew my crueltie,
My falseness and my plain oppression,
    He gave command that I should be
Hangit, and that without confession.

And yet because that I was auld
    His grace thocht pity for to hang me,
But let me wander where I wald,
    Then set my foës for to fang me.

     *   *   *   *

Gude brother Lanceman, Lyndsay's dog,
    Whilk ay has keepit thy lautie,
And never worryit lamb nor hog,
    Pray Luffra, Scudlar and Bawtie
    Of me Bagsche to have pitie,

And provide me ane portion,
    In Dunfermline, where I may dre
Penance for my extortion:

Get by their solicitation
    Ane letter from the Kingis grace,
That I may have collation,
    With fire and candle in the place.
    But I will live short time, alas!
Want I gude fresh flesh for my gammis;
    Betwixt Ashwednesday and Paice,
I must have leave to worrie lambis.

Bawtie, consider well this bill,
    And read this schedule that I send
        you,
And every point thereof fulfil,
    And now in time of mys amend you;
    I pray you that ye nocht pretend you,
To climb ower high, nor do na wrang,
    But from your foes with richt defend
        you,
And take example how I gang.

I was that na man durst come near me,
    Nor put me forth of my lodging;
Na dog durst fra my dinner scare me,
    When I was tender with the King:
    Now every tyke does me down thring,
The whilk before by me were wrangit,
    And swears I serve na other thing,
But in a halter to be hangit.

Thocht ye be hamely with the King,
 Ye, Luffra, Scudlar and Bawtie,
Beware ye do nocht down thring
  Your neighbours thro' authoritie ;
  And your example made by me,
And believe weill ye are but doggis,
  Thocht ye stand in the highest gre,
See ye bite neither lambis nor hoggis.

  *   *   *   *

I took na mair count of ane lord
 Nor I did of ane kitchen knave ;
Thocht every day I made discord,
  I was set up above the lave,
  The gentle hound was to me slave,
And with the Kingis own fingers fed,
  The silly rachis wald I rave :
Thus, for my evil deedis was I dread.

Therefore, Bawtie, look best about,
 When thou art highest with the King,
For then thou standis in greatest doubt,
  Be thou nocht gude of governing :
  Put na puir tyke from his steiding,
Nor yet na silly rachis rave ;
  He sittis above that sees a' thing,
And of ane knight can mak' ane knave.

When I came stepping o'er the floor,
 All rachis great room to me red ;
I of na creature took cure,
  But lap upon the Kingis bed,
  With cloth of gold, tho' it were spread;

For fear ilk freik would stand a far
  With every dog I was so dread,
They tremblit when they heard me near.

     *   *   *   *

  Wald God I were now in Pittarie,
Because I have been so evil deedie :
  Adieu ! I dare na langer tarrie
In dread I waif in till ane widdie.

Lyndsay.

CXXIII

LOVE ME, LOVE MY DOG

INDEED (my Dear) you wrong my Dog in this,
And show yourself to be of crabbèd kind,
That will not let my fawning whelp to kiss
You first, that fain would show his Master's
    mind :
    A Mastiff were more fit for such a one,
    That can not let her Lover's dog alone.

He in his kind for me did seem to sue,
That erst did stand so highly in your grace,
His Master's mind the witty Spaniel knew,
And thought his wonted Mistress was in place :
    But now at last (good faith) I plainly see
    That Dogs more wise than women friendly
    be.

Wherefore since you so cruelly entreat
My whelp, not forcing of his fawning cheer,
You show yourself with pride to be replete,
And to your Friend your nature doth appear :
    The Proverb old is verified in you,
    Love me and Love my Dog, and so adieu !

Both I and he, that silly beast, sustain
For loving well and bearing faithful hearts,
Despitous checks, and rigorous disdain,
Where both hath well deservèd for our parts,
    For Friendship I, for offered service he,
    And yet thou neither lov'st the Dog nor me.
                     Turberville.

CXXIV

THE FAITHFULLEST BEAST

OF any beast none is more faithful found,
Nor yields more pastime in house, plain, or woods,
Nor keeps his Master's person, or his goods,
With greater care than doth the dog or hound.

Command, he thee obeys most readily ;
Strike him, he whines and falls down at thy feet ;
Call him, he leaves his game and comes to thee
With wagging tail, off'ring his service meek.

In summer's heat he follows by thy pace ;
In winter's cold he never leaveth thee ;
In mountains wild he by thee close doth trace ;
In all thy fears and dangers true is he.

Thy friends he loves ; and in thy presence lives
By day ; by night he watcheth faithfully
That thou in peace may'st sleep ; he never
      gives
Good entertainment to thine enemy.

Course, hunt, in hills, in valley, or in plain—
He joys to run and stretch out every limb ;
To please but thee he spareth for no pains,
His hurt (for thee) is greatest good to him.

Sometimes he doth present thee with a Hare,
Sometimes he hunts the Stag, the Fox, the
      Boar,
Another time he baits the Bull and Bear,
And all to make thee sport, and for no more.

If so thou wilt, a Collar he will wear ;
And when thou list to take it off again,
Unto thy feet he croucheth down most fair,
As if thy will were all his good and gain.

In fields abroad he looks unto thy flocks,
Keeping them safe from wolves and other
      beasts ;
And oftentimes he bears away the knocks
Of some odd thief that many a fold infests.

And as he is thy faithful body's guard,
So he is good within a fort or hold,
Against a quick surprise to watch and ward,
And all his hire is bread, musty and old.

Canst thou then such a creature hate and spurn?
Or bar him from such poor and simple food?—
Being so fit and faithful for thy turn,
As no beast else can do thee half such good.

Molle (CAMERARIUS).

CXXV

AMBIGUITY

LAST night you laid it (Madam) in our dish,
How that a maid of ours (whom we must check)
Had broke your bitch's leg, I straight did wish
The baggage rather broken had her neck:
You took my answer well, and all was whish.
But take me right, I meant in that I said,
Your baggage bitch, and not my baggage
maid.

Harington.

CXXVI

IN PRAISE OF BUNGEY

BECAUSE a witty writer of this time
Doth make some mention in a pleasant rhyme
Of Lepidus and of his famous dog,
Thou, Momus, that dost love to scoff and cog,
Prat'st amongst base companions, and giv'st out
That unto me herein is meant a flout.
Hate makes thee blind, Momus, I dare be sworn,
He meant to me his love, to thee his scorn;

Put on thy envious spectacles and see
Whom doth he scorn therein—the dog or me.
The dog is graced, comparèd with great Banks,
Both beasts right famous for their pretty pranks ;
Although in this I grant the dog was worse,
He only fed my pleasure, not my purse ;
Yet that same dog, I may say this and boast it,
He found my purse with gold when I have lost it.
Now for myself, some fools (like thee) may judge
That at the name of Lepidus I grudge ;
No, sure ; so far I think it from disgrace,
I wished it clear to me and to my race.
Lepus or Lepos, I in both have part,
That in my name I bear, this in mine heart.
But, Momus, I persuade myself that no man
Will deign thee such a name, English or Roman.
　　I 'll wage a butt of sack, the best in Bristo,
　　Who calls me Lepid, I will call him Tristo.

Harington.

CXXVII

ON STRIKING HIS WIFE'S DOG

Your little dog that barked as I came by,
I strake by hap so hard, I made him cry,
And straight you put your finger in your eye,
And low'ring sat, and asked the reason why.
Love me and love my dog, thou didst reply :
Love, as both should be loved, I will, said I,
And sealed it with a kiss.　Then by and by

Cleared were the clouds of thy fair frowning sky ;
Thus small events great masteries may try.
    For I by this do at their meaning guess,
    That beat a whelp afore a lioness.

Harington.

CXXVIII

THE MASTIFF-WORRYING FLY

So have I seen ere this a silly fly
With mastiff dog in summer's heat to play,
Sometimes to sting him in his nose or eye,
Sometimes about his grisly jaws to stay,
And buzzing round about his ears to fly,
He snaps in vain, for still she whips away,
    And oft so long she dallies in this sort,
    Till one snap comes and marreth all her sport.

Harington.

CXXIX

A TRIAL OF ENDURANCE

E'EN as a mastiff fell, whom grewnd more fell
Hath tired, and in his throat now fastened hath
His cruel fangs, yet doth in vain rebel,
Though under him, and seeks to do some skath :
For still the grewnd prevails, and doth excel
In force of breath, though not in rage and wrath.

Harington.

CXXX

THE DANCING DOG

Then Ball, my cut-tailed cur, and I begin to play :
He o'er my sheephook leaps, now th' one, now
    th' other way,
Then on his hinder feet he doth himself advance,
I tune, and to my note my lively dog will dance.

Drayton.

CXXXI

FAREWELL TO WHITEFOOT

He called his dog (that sometime had the praise)
Whitefoot, well known to all that keep the plain,
That many a wolf had worried in his days,
A better cur there never followed swain ;
      Which, though as he his master's sorrows
        knew,
      Wagged his cut tail, his wretched plight
        to rue.

'Poor cur,' quoth he, and him therewith did stroke ;
' Go to our cote, and there thyself repose,
Thou with thine age, my heart with sorrow broke,
Be gone e'er death my restless eyes do close,
      The time is come thou must thy master
        leave,
      Whom the vile world shall never more
        deceive.'

Drayton.

CXXXII

HELENA'S HUMBLE PETITION

I AM your spaniel; and, Demetrius,
The more you beat me, I will fawn on you:
Use me but as your spaniel, spurn me, strike me,
Neglect me, lose me; only give me leave,
Unworthy as I am, to follow you.
What worser place can I beg in your love
(And yet a place of high respect with me)
Than to be usèd as you use your dog?

Shakespeare.

CXXXIII

LEAR AND THE DOGS

LEAR

THE little dogs and all,
Tray, Blanch, and Sweetheart, see, they bark at
me.

EDGAR

Tom will throw his head at them.—
Avaunt, you curs!
Be thy mouth or black or white,
Tooth that poisons if it bite;
Mastiff, greyhound, mongrel grim,
Hound or spaniel, brach or lym,

Or bobtail tyke or trundel-tail,—
Tom will make them weep and wail:
For, with throwing thus my head,
Dogs leap the hatch, and all are fled.

Shakespeare.

CXXXIV

DIFFERENCES IN DOGS

Ay, in the catalogue ye go for men;
As hounds, and greyhounds, mongrels, spaniels,
    curs,
Shoughs, water-rugs, and demi-wolves are clepped
All by the name of dogs: the valued file
Distinguishes the swift, the slow, the subtle,
The housekeeper, the hunter, every one
According to the gift which bounteous nature
Hath in him closed; whereby he does receive
Particular addition from the bill
That writes them all alike: and so of men.

Shakespeare.

CXXXV

MISANTHROPOS

I am Misanthropos, and hate mankind.
For thy part, I do wish thou wert a dog,
That I might love thee something.

Shakespeare.

CXXXVI

IN CINEAM

Thou doggèd Cineas, hated like a dog,
For still thou grumblest like a masty dog,
Compar'st thyself to nothing but a dog;
Thou say'st thou art as weary as a dog,
As angry, sick, and hungry as a dog,
As dull and melancholy as a dog,
As lazy, sleepy, idle as a dog.
But why dost thou compare thee to a dog
In that for which all men despise a dog?
I will compare thee better to a dog;
Thou art as fair and comely as a dog,
Thou art as true and honest as a dog,
Thou art as kind and liberal as a dog,
Thou art as wise and valiant as a dog.
But, Cineas, I have often heard thee tell,
Thou art as like thy father as may be:
'Tis like enough; and, faith, I like it well;
But I am glad thou art not like to me.

Davies.

CXXXVII

THE DOG STAR

When her dear bosom clips
That little cur, which fawns to touch her lips,
Or when it is his hap
To lie lapped in her lap,

Oh it grows noon with me,
With hotter pointed beams
I burn, than those are which the sun forth
    streams,
When piercing lightning his rays called may be :
And as I muse how I to those extremes
Am brought, I find no cause, except that she
In love's bright zodiac having traced each room,
To the hot Dog-star now at last is come.

Drummond.

CXXXVIII

A COMEDY

Philos of his dog doth brag
For having many feats :
The while the cur undoes his bag,
And all his dinner eats.

JOCKIE

THE other day it fell,
Leaving my sheep to graze on yonder plain,
I went to fill my bottle at the well,
And, ere I could return, two lambs were slain.

PHILOS

Then was thy dog ill-taught, or else asleep ;
Such curs as those shall never watch my sheep.

WILLIE

Yet Philos hath a dog not of the best;
He seems too lazy, and will take no pains;
More fit to lie at home and take his rest,
Than catch a wandering sheep upon the plains.

JOCKIE

'Tis true indeed; and, Philos, wot ye what?
I think he plays the fox, he grows so fat.

PHILOS

Yet hath not Jockie, nor yet Willie, seen
A dog more nimble than is this of mine,
Nor any of the fox more heedful been
When in the shade I slept, or list to dine.
   And, though I say't, hath better tricks in store
   Than both of yours, or twenty couples more.

How often have the maidens strove to take him!
When he hath crossed the plain to bark at
    crows!
How many lasses have I known to make him
Garlands to gird his neck, with which he goes
Vaunting along the lands so wondrous trim,
That not a dog of yours durst bark at him!
And when I list (as often time I use)
To tune a hornpipe, or a morris-dance,
The dog (as he by nature could not choose)
Seeming asleep before, will leap and dance.

WILLIE

Belike your dog came of a pedlar's brood,
Or Philos' music is exceeding good.

PHILOS

I boast not of his kin, nor of my reed
(Though of my reed, and him I well may boast),
Yet if you will adventure that some meed
Shall be to him that is in action most,
    As for a collar of shrill sounding bells,
    My dog shall strive with yours, or any's else.

JOCKIE

Philos, in truth, I must confess your Wag
(For so you call him) hath of tricks good store,
To steal the victuals from his master's bag
More cunningly, I ne'er saw dog before.
    See, Willie, see! I prithee, Philos, note
    How fast thy bread and cheese goes down his
        throat.

WILLIE

Now, Philos, see how mannerly your cur,
Your well-taught dog, that hath so many tricks,
Devours your dinner.

PHILOS

                        I wish 'twere a bur
To choke the mongrel!

JOCKIE

See how he licks
Your butter-box; by Pan, I do not meanly
Love Philos' dog, that loves to be so cleanly.

PHILOS

Well flouted, Jockie.

WILLIE

Philos, run amain,
For in your scrip he now hath thrust his head
So far, he cannot get it forth again;
See how he blindfold strags along the mead;
   And at your scrip your bottle hangs, I think:
   He loves your meat, but cares not for your drink.

JOCKIE

Ay, so it seems: and Philos now may go
Unto the wood, or home for other cheer.

PHILOS

'Twere better he had never served me so,
Sweet meat, sour sauce, he shall a-buy it dear.
What, must he be aforehand with his master?

WILLIE

Only in kindness he would be your taster.

PHILOS

Well, Willie, you may laugh, and urge my spleen:
But by my hook I swear he shall it rue,
And had fared better had he fasting been.
But I must home for my allowance new.

Browne.

CXXXIX

AGRIPPA'S PUG

Quoth Hudibras—
Agrippa kept a Stygian pug,
I' th' garb and habit of a dog,
That was his tutor, and the cur
Read to th' occult philosopher,
And taught him subtly to maintain
All other sciences are vain.

To this quoth Sidrophello, Sir,
Agrippa was no conjurer,
Nor Paracelsus, no, nor Behmen;
Nor was the dog a cacodæmon,
But a true dog that would show tricks
For th' Emperor, and leap o'er sticks;
Would fetch and carry, was more civil
Than other dogs, and yet no devil.

Butler.

CXL

THE IRISH GREYHOUND

Behold this Creature's form and state,
Which Nature therefore did create,
That to the World might be expressed
What mien there can be in a Beast;
And that we in this shape may find
A Lion of another kind,

For this Heroic beast does seem
In Majesty to Rival him,
And yet vouchsafes to Man to show
Both service and submission too.
From whence we this distinction have,
That Beast is fierce, but that is brave.
This Dog hath so himself subdued
That hunger cannot make him rude :
And his behaviour does confess
True Courage dwells with Gentleness.
With sternest Wolves he dares engage,
And acts on them successful rage.
Yet too much courtesy may chance
To put him out of countenance.
When in his opposer's blood,
Fortune hath made his virtue good ;
This Creature from an act so brave
Grows not more sullen, but more grave.
Man's Guard he would be, not his sport,
Believing he hath ventured for 't ;
But yet no blood or shed or spent
Can ever make him insolent.
Few men of him to do great things have learned,
And, when th' are done, to be so unconcerned.

Katherine Philips.

HIS MISTRESS' DOG

Thou, happy creature, art secure
From all the torments we endure ;

Despair, ambition, jealousy,
Lost friends, nor love, disquiet thee ;
A sullen prudence drew thee hence
From noise, fraud, and impertinence.
Though life essayed the surest wile,
Gilding itself with Laura's smile ;
How didst thou scorn life's meaner charms,
Thou who couldst break from Laura's arms !
Poor Cynic ! still methinks I hear
Thy awful murmurs in my ear ;
As when on Laura's lap you lay,
Chiding the worthless crowd away.
How fondly human passions turn !
What we then envied, now we mourn.

Roscommon.

CXLII

THE DOG IN THE MANGER

An envious Dog that Brooding lay,
Upon a Crib Replete with Hay,
Snarls at the Ox that thither came,
An eager appetite to tame.
And forced him back, incensed, whereat
He on the Dog invokes this Fate :—
May the Just Gods so punish thee,
As thy Rude Spleen hath injured me,
Who Does prohibit me the meat,
Whereon thy Self disdains to eat.

Aphra Behn (Æsop).

CXLIII

THE DOG AND THE SHADOW

THE Dog who with his prey the River swam
Saw his own laden Image in the stream.
The wishing Cur grown covetous of all,
To catch the Shadow lets the Substance fall.

Aphra Behn (ÆSOP).

CXLIV

THE HOME-LOVING DOG

THE lonely fox roams far abroad,
On secret rapine bent, and midnight fraud ;
Now haunts the cliff, now traverses the lawn,
And flies the hated neighbourhood of man :
While the kind spaniel, or the faithful hound,
Likest that fox in shape and species found,
Refuses through these cliffs and lawns to roam,
Pursues the noted path, and covets home ;
Does with kind joy domestic faces meet,
Take what the glutted child denies to eat,
And, dying, licks his long-loved master's feet.

Prior.

CXLV

UPON THE HORRID PLOT

DISCOVERED BY HARLEQUIN, THE BISHOP OF
ROCHESTER'S FRENCH DOG

(A Dialogue between a Whig and a Tory)

I ASKED a Whig the other night
How came this wicked plot to light?
He answered that a *dog* of late
Informed a minister of state.
Said I, 'From thence I nothing know,
For are not all informers so?
A villain who his friend betrays
We style him by no other phrase;
And so a perjured dog denotes
Porter and Prendergast and Oates,
And forty others I could name.'

WHIG

But, you must know, this dog was lame.

TORY

A weighty argument indeed!
Your evidence was *lame*: proceed—
Come, help your *lame dog o'er the style.*

WHIG

Sir, you mistake me all this while.
I mean a dog (without a joke)
Can howl and bark, but never spoke.

TORY

I'm still to speak which dog you mean,
Whether cur Plunkett, or whelp Skean,
An English or an Irish hound ;
Or t'other puppy that was drowned ;
Or Mason, that abandoned bitch—
Then pray be free, and tell me which :
For every stander by was marking
That all the noise they made was barking.
You pay them well ; the *dogs* have got
Their dog-heads in a porridge pot :
And 'twas but just ; for wise men say
That *every dog must have his day*.
Dog Walpole laid a quart of nog on't,
He'd either make a hog or dog on't ;
And looked, since he has got his wish,
As if he had *thrown down a dish*.
Yet this I dare foretell you from it,
He'll soon return to his own vomit.

WHIG

Besides this horrid plot was found
By Neynoe after he was drowned.

TORY

Why then the proverb is not right,
Since you can teach *dead dogs* to bite.

WHIG

I proved my proposition full,
But Jacobites are strangely dull.

Now let me tell you plainly, sir,
Our witness is a real cur,
A dog of spirit for his years,
Has twice two legs, two hanging ears;
His name is Harlequin, I wot,
And that's a name in every plot;
Resolved to save the British nation,
Though French by birth and education;
His correspondence plainly dated,
Was all deciphered and translated;
His answers were exceeding pretty
Before the secret wise committee;
Confessed as plain as he could bark,
Then with his fore-foot set his mark.

TORY

Then all this while I have been bubbled,
I thought it was a *dog in doublet*;
The matter now no longer sticks,
For statesmen never want *dog-tricks*.
But since it was a real cur,
And not a dog in metaphor,
I give you joy of the report
That he's to have a place at court.

WHIG

Yes, and a place he will grow rich in—
A turnspit in the royal kitchen.
Sir, to be plain, I tell you what,
We had occasion for a plot:
And, when we found the dog begin it,
We guessed the Bishop's foot was in it.

TORY

I own it was a dangerous project,
And you have proved it by *dog-logic*.
Sure such intelligence between
A dog and bishop ne'er was seen
Till you began to change the breed ;
Your bishops all are *dogs* indeed !

Swift.

CXLVI

ADVICE TO A DOG PAINTER

HAPPIEST of the spaniel race,
Painter, with thy colours grace :
Draw his forehead large and high,
Draw his blue and humid eye ;
Draw his neck so smooth and round,
Little neck with ribands bound ;
And the *musely* swelling breast
Where the Loves and Graces rest ;
And the spreading even back,
Soft, and sleek, and glossy black ;
And the tail that gently twines,
Like the tendrils of the vines ;
And the silky twisted hair,
Shadowing thick the *velvet* ear ;
Velvet ears, which, hanging low,
O'er the *veiny* temples flow.

Swift.

CXLVII

THE DOGS OF NILE

LIKE the dogs of Nile be wise ;
Who, taught by instinct how to shun
The crocodile, that lurking lies,
Run as they drink, and drink and run.

Swift.

CXLVIII

ON THE COLLAR OF TIGER

PRAY steal me not ; I 'm Mrs. Dingley's,
Whose heart in this four-footed thing lies.

Swift.

CXLIX

LOVER'S LOGIC

My Bawty is a cur I dearly like,
Till he yowled fair she strak the poor dumb tyke :
If I had filled a nook within her breast,
She wad have shawn mair kindness to my beast.

Ramsay.

CL

TRAY, THE EXEMPLAR

My dog (the trustiest of his kind)
With gratitude inflames my mind;
I mark his true, his faithful way,
And in my service copy Tray.

Gay.

CLI

A COLLAR INSCRIPTION

I am his Highness' dog at Kew;
Pray tell me, sir, whose dog are you?

Pope.

CLII

A SIMPLE FAITH

Lo, the poor Indian! whose untutored mind
Sees God in clouds, or hears him in the wind;
His soul proud science never taught to stray
Far as the solar walk, or milky way;
Yet simple nature to his hope has given,
Behind the cloud-topped hill, a humbler heaven;

Some safer world, in depths of woods embraced,
Some happier island in the watery waste,
Where slaves once more their native land behold,
No friends torment, no Christians thirst for gold:
To be, contents his natural desire;
He asks no angel's wing, no seraph's fire;
But thinks, admitted to that equal sky,
His faithful dog shall bear him company.

Pope.

CLIII

ALL-ACCOMPLISHED ROVER

Man, of precarious science vain,
Treats other creatures with disdain;
Nor Pug nor Shock has common sense,
Nor even Poll the least pretence,
Though she prates better than us all,
To be accounted rational.
The brute creation here below,
It seems, is Nature's puppet show;
But clock-work all, and mere machine,
What can these idle gimcracks mean?
Ye world-makers of Gresham Hall,
Dog Rover shall confute you all;
Shall prove that every reasoning brute
Like Ben of Bangor can dispute,
Can apprehend, judge, syllogise;
Or like proud Bentley criticise:

At a moot point, or odd disaster,
Is often wiser than his master.
He may mistake sometimes, 'tis true,—
None are infallible but you.
The dog whom nothing can mislead
Must be a dog of parts indeed.

Rover, as heralds are agreed,
Well-born, and of the setting breed,
Ranged high, was stout, of nose acute,
A very learned and courteous brute.
In parallel lines his ground he beat,
Not such as in one centre meet,
In those let blundering doctors deal,
His were exactly parallel.
When tainted gales the game betray,
Down close he sinks, and eyes his prey,
Though different passions tempt his soul,
True as the needle to the pole,
He keeps his point, and panting lies,
The floating net above him flies,
Then, dropping, sweeps the fluttering
    prize.
Nor this his only excellence :
When surly farmers took offence,
And the rank corn the sport denied,
Still faithful to his master's side,
A thousand pretty pranks he played,
And cheerful each command obeyed ;
Humble his mind, though great his wit,
Would lug a pig, or turn the spit ;

Would fetch and carry, leap o'er sticks,
And forty such diverting tricks.
Nor Partridge nor wife Gadbury,
Could find lost goods so soon as he;
Bid him go back a mile or more
And seek the glove you hid before,
Still his unerring nose would wind it,
If above ground, was sure to find it,
Whimpering for joy his master greet,
And humbly lay it at his feet.

Somervile.

CLIV

THE DOG INCOG.

Calm though not mean, courageous without rage,
Serious not dull, and without thinking sage;
Pleased at the lot that nature has assigned,
Snarl as I list, and freely bark my mind;
As churchman wrangle not with jarring spite,
Nor statesmanlike caressing whom I bite;
View all the canine kind with equal eyes,
I dread no mastiff, and no cur despise,
True from the first, and faithful to the end,
I balk no mistress, and forsake no friend.
My days and nights one equal tenour keep,
Fast but to eat, and only wake to sleep.
Thus stealing along life I live *incog.*,
A very plain and downright honest dog.

William Hamilton (of Bangour).

CLV

REVENGE

Lo, when two dogs are fighting in the streets,
With a third dog one of the two dogs meets;
With angry teeth he bites him to the bone,
And this dog smarts for what that dog has done.

Fielding.

CLVI

THE WANING HONEYMOON

FULL oft, unknowing what they did,
They called in adventitious aid.
A faithful fav'rite dog ('twas thus
With Tobit and Telemachus)
Amused their steps; and for a while
They viewed his gambols with a smile.

Whitehead.

CLVII

TO A YOUNG LADY'S DOG.

PRETTY sportive happy creature,
Full of life, and full of play,
Taught to live by faithful Nature,
Never canst thou miss thy way.

By her dictates kind instructed,
Thou avoid'st each real smart ;
We, by other rules conducted,
Lose our joy to show our art.

Undisguised, each reigning passion,
When thou mov'st or look'st we see :
Were the same with us the fashion,
Happy mortals would we be !

May her favour still pursue thee,
Who proposed thee for my theme ;
Till superior charms subdue thee,
And inspire a nobler flame.

In each other blessed and blessing,
Years of pleasure let them live ;
Each all active worth possessing,
Earth admires or heaven can give.

Blacklock.

CLVIII

THE GALLIC LAP-DOG

IF you would scan the beauties of a pup ;
The page is out, and not the total up.

Elphinston (MARTIAL).

CLIX

ISSA'S PORTRAIT

Issa, perter than the sparrow,
That poor Lesbia's soul could harrow ;
Issa, purer than the love,
Of Ianthis' billing dove ;
Issa, than a maid more fond ;
Issa, Indian gems beyond ;
Issa, most enchanting chub !
Pup, the darling of my Pub !
She can speak her wants and woes :
She both joy and sorrow knows.
On his neck her bed she makes ;
And her silken slumbers takes :
Nay, so soft does Somnus ply,
No one can detect a sigh.

    *   *   *   *

Lest the fatal final day
Rap his charmer all away ;
Publius, prescient of his woe,
Bade her by the pencil glow.
In the image, eye the elf
Liker far than in herself.
Bring together, or dispart,
Nature's, and the child of art :
Nature says, they both are mine ;
Art both vindicates divine.

Elphinston (MARTIAL).

CLX

INSULAR PREJUDICE

A snub-nosed dog, to fat inclined,
Of the true hogan-mogan kind,
The favourite of an English dame,
Mynheer Van Trumpo was his name,
One morning as he chanced to range
Met honest Towzer on the 'Change.

*   *   *   *

' An English dog can't take an airing
But foreign scoundrels must be staring.
I 'd have your French dogs and your Spanish,
And all your Dutch and all your Danish,
By which our species is confounded,
Be hanged, be poisoned, and be drownèd ;
No mercy on the race suspected,
Greyhounds from Italy excepted.

' Well, of all dogs it stands confessed
Your English bull-dogs are the best,
I say it, and will set my hand to 't,
Camden records it, and I 'll stand to 't.'

Smart.

CLXI

BEAU AND THE BIRD

A spaniel, Beau, that fares like you,
   Well-fed, and at his ease,
Should wiser be than to pursue
   Each trifle that he sees.

But you have killed a tiny bird,
 Which flew not till to-day,
Against my orders, whom you heard
 Forbidding you the prey.

Nor did you kill that you might eat,
 And ease a doggish pain,
For him, though chased with furious heat,
 You left where he was slain.

Nor was he of the thievish sort,
 Or one whom blood allures,
But innocent was all his sport
 Whom you have torn for yours.

My dog! what remedy remains,
 Since, teach you all I can,
I see you, after all my pains,
 So much resemble man?

      Cowper.

CLXII

BEAU'S REPLY

Sir, when I flew to seize the bird
 In spite of your command,
A louder voice than yours I heard,
 And harder to withstand.

You cried—forbear—but in my breast
 A mightier cried—proceed—
'Twas nature, sir, whose strong behest
 Impelled me to the deed.

Yet much as nature I respect,
    I ventured once to break
(As you perhaps may recollect)
    Her precept for your sake ;

And when your linnet on a day,
    Passing his prison door,
Had fluttered all his strength away,
    And panting pressed the floor,

Well knowing him a sacred thing,
    Not destined to my tooth,
I only kissed his ruffled wing,
    And licked the feathers smooth.

Let my obedience then excuse
    My disobedience now,
Nor some reproot yourself refuse
    From your aggrieved Bow-wow :

If killing birds be such a crime
    (Which I can hardly see),
What think you, sir, of killing time
    With verse addressed to me ?

Cowper.

CLXIII

A FROLIC IN THE SNOW

Forth goes the woodman, leaving unconcerned
The cheerful haunts of man, to wield the axe
And drive the wedge in yonder forest drear,
From morn to eve his solitary task.

Shaggy and lean and shrewd, with pointed ears
And tail cropped short, half lurcher and half cur,
His dog attends him.   Close behind his heel
Now creeps he slow, and now with many a frisk,
Wide-scamp'ring, snatches up the drifted snow
With iv'ry teeth, or ploughs it with his snout ;
Then shakes his powdered coat, and barks for joy.
Heedless of all his pranks, the sturdy churl
Moves right toward the mark.

Cowper.

CLXIV

OLD FRIENDS

THE old shepherd's dog, like his master, was
    grey ;
  His teeth all departed, and feeble his tongue ;
Yet where'er Corin went, he was followed by
    Tray ;
  Thus happy through life did they hobble along.

When fatigued, on the grass the shepherd would
    lie
  For a nap in the sun—'midst his slumbers so
    sweet,
His faithful companion crawled constantly nigh,
  Placed his head on his lap, or lay down at his
    feet.

When winter was heard on the hill and the plain,
　　And torrents descended, and cold was the wind,
If Corin went forth 'midst the tempests and rain
　　Tray scorned to be left in the chimney behind.

At length in the straw Tray made his last bed ;
　　For vain against death is the stoutest en-
　　　deavour ;
To lick Corin's hand he reared up his weak head,
　　Then fell back, closed his eyes, and, ah ! closed
　　　them for ever.

Not long after Tray did the shepherd remain,
　　Who oft o'er his grave with true sorrow would
　　　bend ;
And when dying thus feebly was heard the poor
　　swain :
　　' O, bury me, neighbours, beside my old
　　　friend.'

　　　　　　　　　　　　Peter Pindar (*Wolcot*).

CLXV

THE PUPS AND THE ALLIGATOR

THUS on a bank, upon a summer's day,
　　Of some fair stream of East or Western Ind,
When puppies join in wanton play,
　　Free from the slightest fear of being skinned ;

If from that stream, which all so placid flows,
A sly old alligator pokes his nose ;
P'rhaps with a wish to taste a slice of cur ;
At once the dogs are off upon the spur ;
Nor once behind them cast a courtly look,
To compliment the monarch of the brook.

Peter Pindar (*Wolcot*).

CLXVI

THE BLIND MAN'S DOG

By nature fierce, at length subdued and mild
To each kind office of a duteous child,
Who a dark sire guides through the pressing
   throng :
See how yon terrier gently leads along
The feeble beggar to his 'customed stand,
With piteous tale to woo the bounteous hand ;
In willing bonds, but master of the way,
Ne'er leads that trusted friend his charge astray,
With slow, soft step, as conscious of his care,
As if his own deep sorrows formed the prayer ;
Should yielding charity the scrip supply,
Though hunger pressed, untouched the boon
   would lie ;
Eyes to the blind, he notes the passing thief,
And guards the good Samaritan's relief ;
A faithful steward 'midst unbounded power,
Patient he waits the home-returning hour ;

Then reconducts his master to his shed,
And grateful banquets on the coarsest bread.
And were that cheerless shed by Fortune placed
In the deep cavern, on the naked waste,
The sport of every storm, unroofed and bare,
This faithful slave would find a palace there,
Would feel the labours of his love o'erpaid
Near to his monarch master's pillow laid;
Unchanged by change of circumstance or place:
Oh sacred lesson to a prouder race!

Pratt.

CLXVII

PROVERBIAL PHILOSOPHY

A DOG starved at his master's gate
Predicts the ruin of the State.

The beggar's dog, the widow's cat,
Feed them and thou shalt grow fat.

Blake.

CLXVIII

GROWN OLD TOGETHER

THE dog and I are both grown old;
  On these wild downs we watch all day;
He looks in my face when the wind blows cold,
  And thus methinks I hear him say:

'The grey stone circlet is below,
　The village smoke is at our feet ;
We nothing hear but the sailing crow,
　And wandering flocks, that roam and bleat.

Far off the early horseman hies,
　In shower or sunshine rushing on ;
Yonder the dusty whirlwind flies ;
　The distant coach is seen and gone.

Though solitude around is spread,
　Master, alone thou shalt not be ;
And when the turf is on thy head,
　I only shall remember thee ! '

I marked his look of faithful care,
　I placed my hand on his shaggy side :
'There is a sun that shines above,
　A sun that shines on both,' I cried.

Bowles.

CLXIX

TO ERR IS HUMAN

Though faithful to a proverb we regard
The midnight chieftain of the farmer's yard,
Beneath whose guardianship all hearts rejoice,
Woke by the echo of his hollow voice ;
Yet as the Hound may fault'ring quit the pack,
Snuff the foul scent, and hasten yelping back ;

And e'en the docile Pointer know disgrace,
Thwarting the gen'ral instinct of his race;
E'en so the Mastiff, or the meaner cur,
At times will from the path of duty err
(A pattern of fidelity by day,
By night a murderer, lurking for his prey),
And round the pastures or the fold will creep,
And, coward-like, attack the peaceful sheep.
Alone the wanton mischief he pursues,
Alone in reeking blood his jaw imbrues;
Chasing amain his frightened victims round,
Till death in wild confusion strews the ground;
Then, wearied out, to kennel sneaks away,
And licks his guilty paws till break of day.

Bloomfield.

CLXX

MY AULD HECTOR

COME, my auld towzy trusty friend,
   What gars ye look sae dung wi' wae?
D' ye think my favour 's at an end
   Because thy head is turnin' grey?

Although thy strength begins to fail,
   Its best was spent in serving me;
An' can I grudge thy wee bit meal,
   Some comfort in thy age to gie?

For mony a day, frae sun to sun,
　We've toiled fu' hard wi' ane anither;
An' mony a thousand mile thou'st run
　To keep my thraward flocks thegither.

To nae thrawn boy nor naughty wife
　Shall thy auld banes become a drudge;
At cats an' callans a' thy life
　Thou ever bor'st a mortal grudge;

An' whiles thy surly look declared
　Thou lo'ed the women warst of a'
Because my love wi' thee they shared—
　A matter out o' right or law.

When sittin' wi' my bonnie Meg,
　Mair happy than a prince could be,
Thou placed thee by her other leg,
　An' watched her wi' a jealous e'e.

An' then at ony start or flare
　Thou wadst hae worried furiouslye;
While I was forced to curse an' swear
　Afore thou wadst forbidden be.

Yet wad she clasp thy towzy paw;
　Thy gruesome grips were never skaithly;
An' thou than her hast been mair true,
　An' truer than the friend that gae thee.

Ah me! o' fashion, self, an' pride,
　Mankind hae read me sic a lecture;
But yet it's a' in part repaid
　By thee, my faithful grateful Hector!

O'er past imprudence oft alane
   I 've shed the saut and silent tear ;
Then sharin' a' my grief an' pain,
   My poor auld friend came snoovin' near.

For a' the days we 've sojourned here,
   An' they 've been neither fine nor few,
That thought possest thee year to year,
   That a' my griefs arase frae you.

Wi' waesome face an' hingin' head
   Thou wadst hae pressed thee to my knee ;
While I thy looks as weel could read
   As thou hadst said in words to me :

O my dear master, dinna greet ;
   What hae I ever done to vex thee ?
See here I 'm cowrin' at your feet—
   Just take my life if I perplex thee.

For a' my toil, my wee drap meat
   Is a' the wage I ask of thee ;
For whilk I 'm oft obliged to wait
   Wi' hungry wame an' patient e'e.

Whatever wayward course ye steer,
   Whatever sad mischance o'ertake ye,
Man, here is ane will hald ye dear !
   Man, here is ane will ne'er forsake ye ! '

Yes, my puir beast, though friends me scorn,
   Whom mair than life I valued dear,
An' thraw me out to fight forlorn,
   Wi' ills my heart do hardly bear,

While I hae thee to bear a part—
    My health, my plaid, an' heezle rung,
I 'll scorn the unfeeling haughty heart,
    The saucy look, and slanderous tongue.

   *   *   *   *

An' hear me, Hector, thee I 'll trust,
    As far as thou hast wit an' skill ;
Sae will I ae sweet lovely breast,
    To me a balm for every ill.

To these my trust shall ever turn,
    While I have reason truth to scan ;
But ne'er beyond my mother's son
    To aught that bears the shape o' man.

I ne'er could thole thy cravin' face,
    Nor when ye pattit on my knee ;
Though in a far an' unco place
    I 've whiles been forced to beg for thee.

Even now I 'm in my master's power,
    Where my regard may scarce be shown ;
But ere I 'm forced to gie thee o'er,
    When thou art auld an' senseless grown,

I 'll get a cottage o' my ain,
    Some wee bit cannie, lonely biel',
Where thy auld heart shall rest fu' fain,
    An' share wi' me my humble meal.

Thy post shall be to guard the door
    Wi' gousty bark, whate'er betides ;
Of cats an' hens to clear the floor,
    An' bite the flaes that vex thy sides.

When my last bannock's on the hearth,
　Of that thou sanna want thy share ;
While I hae house or hauld on earth,
　My Hector shall hae shelter there.

An' should grim death thy noddle save,
　Till he has made an end o' me ;
Ye'll lye a wee while on the grave
　O' ane wha aye was kind to thee.

There's nane alive will miss me mair ;
　An' though in words thou canst not wail,
On a' the claes thy master ware,
　I ken thou'lt smell an' wag thy tail.

If e'er I'm forced wi' thee to part,
　Which will be sair against my will,
I'll sometimes mind thy honest heart
　As lang as I can climb a hill.

Come, my auld towzy trusty friend,
　Let's speed to Queensb'ry's lofty height ;
All worldly cares we'll leave behind,
　An' onward look to days more bright.

Hogg.

CLXXI

THE JEALOUS TWAIN

At either's feet a trusty squire,
Pandour and Camp, with eyes of fire,
Jealous, each other's motions viewed
And scarce suppressed their ancient feud.

Scott.

TO A SPANIEL

No, Daisy, lift not up thine ear,
It is not she whose steps draw near.
Tuck under thee that leg, for she
Continues yet beyond the sea,
And thou may'st whimper in thy sleep
These many days, and start and weep.

Landor.

MY ONLY FRIENDS

My heart grows sick when home I come—
May God the thought forgive!
If 'twere not for my cat and dog
I think I could not live.
My cat and dog when I come home
Run out to welcome me;
She, mewing with her tail on end,
While wagging his comes he.
They listen for my homeward steps,
My smothered sob they hear,
When down my heart sinks, deathly down,
Because my home is near.

　　　*　　　*　　　*　　　*

Why come they not?   They do not come
My breaking heart to meet;
A heavier darkness on me falls,
I cannot lift my feet.
Oh, yes, they come—they never fail
To listen for my sighs;
My poor heart brightens when it meets
The sunshine of their eyes.
Again they come to meet me—God!
Wilt thou the thought forgive?
If 'twere not for my cat and dog
I think I could not live.

*　　　*　　　*　　　*

My playful cat and honest dog
Are all the friends I have.

Elliott.

CLXXIV

TO TRAY—STOLEN

Ah! whither art thou gone, poor Tray?
　　Ah! whither art thou gone?
And dost thou tread on English land,
Or dost thou on a foreign strand
　　Pour forth thy dismal moan?

Ah! what avails thy beauty, Tray?
　　Ah! what avails thee there?
Thy coat with richest red bedight,
Commingling with the purest white,
　　Thy wiry length of hair!

Ah ! what avails thy beauty, Tray ?
    Ah ! what avails thee now ?
The spotted nose, the feathered feet,
The ears beneath the chin that meet,
    The frown that decks thy brow !

Ah ! fatal were thy beauties, Tray !
    ' Fatally fair ' thy face !
Now stranger hands that nose shall pat,
And unaccustomed voices chat
    Of each peculiar grace.

O ! be thou faithful still, poor Tray !
    And sulk as thou wert wont ;
Ere he whom, in a generous fit,
Nature made painter, poet, wit,
    First led thee forth to hunt.

O ! tease thy thievish owner, Tray !
    O ! tease the plunderer well !
Noisy or mute mistime thy notes,
Soil stockings, garters, petticoats,
    Revolt, resist, rebel !

Revolt, resist, rebel, good Tray !
    And tease his soul amain !
So shall he own the high behest,
That honesty still prospers best,
    And send thee home again.

Mary Russell Mitford.

RUDE RANGER REBUKED

'Then you're so rude!—when people call,
    And your good leave outstay,
You go and stick yourself before 'em
Bolt upright—outraging decorum—
    To beg they'll go away.

'Tis true, they don't quite comprehend
    Your meaning—but I do ;
And when they call you " civil creature " !
And praise your sweet obliging nature—
    Ranger!—I blush for you—'

' Why, mistress ! sure I 've heard you say,
    " Good heavens !—I 'm almost dead—
Those people stayed so!"'—' Come, no sneering–
When they were fairly out of hearing,
    No matter what I said.'

Caroline Bowles Southey.

ON TRUST

My poor old Chloe ! gentle playfellow,
Most patient, most enduring was thy love ;
To restless childhood's teasing fondness proof
And its tormenting ingenuity.
Methinks I see thee in some corner stuck,
In most unnatural position, bolt upright,

With rueful looks and drooping ears forlorn,
Thy two fore-paws, to hold my father's cane—
Converted to a musket—cramped across.
Then wert thou posted like a sentinel
Till numbers ten were slowly counted o'er—
That welcome tenth! the signal sound to thee
Of penance done and liberty regained!
Down went the cane and from thy corner forth
With uproar wild and madly frolic joy,
Bounding aloft, and wheeling round and round,
With mirth inviting antics, didst thou spring.

Caroline Bowles Southey.

CLXXVII

THE WATCH-DOG'S HONEST BARK

'Tis sweet to hear the watch-dog's honest bark
    Bay deep-mouthed welcome as we draw near
      home ;
'Tis sweet to know there is an eye will mark
    Our coming, and look brighter when we
      come.

Byron.

CLXXVIII

MY BLOODHOUND

Come, Herod, my hound, from the stranger's floor !
Old friend,—we must wander the world once more !
For no one now liveth to welcome us back :
So, come !—let us speed on our fated track.

What matter the region,—what matter the
    weather,
So you and I travel, till death, together?
And in death?—why e'en there I may still be
    found
By the side of my beautiful, black bloodhound.

We've traversed the desert, we've traversed the
    sea,
And we've trod on the heights where the eagles
    be;
Seen Tartar, and Arab, and swart Hindoo;
(How thou pull'dst down the deer in those skies
    of blue!)
No joy did divide us; no peril could part
The man from his friend of the noble heart;
Ay, his friend; for where shall there ever be found
A friend like his resolute, fond bloodhound?

What, Herod, old hound! dost remember the day
When I fronted the wolves, like a stag at bay?
When downwards they galloped to where we stood,
Whilst I staggered from dread in the dark pine
    wood?
Dost remember their howlings? their horrible
    speed?
God, God! how I prayed for a friend in need!
And—he came! Ah! 'twas then, my dear Herod,
    I found
That the best of all friends was my bold blood-
    hound.

Men tell us, dear friend, that a noble hound
Must for ever be lost in the worthless ground ;
Yet courage, fidelity, love (they say)
Bear man, as on wings, to his skies away ;
Well, Herod—go tell them whatever may be
I 'll hope I may ever be found by thee :
If in sleep, then in sleep ; if with skies around,
May'st thou follow e'en thither—my dear blood-
    hound.

Barry Cornwall (Procter).

CLXXIX

A GUARDIAN AT THE GATE

THE dog beside the threshold lies,
Mocking sleep, with half-shut eyes—
With head crouched down upon his feet,
Till strangers pass his sunny seat—
Then quick he pricks his ears to hark,
And bustles up to growl and bark ;
While boys in fear stop short their song,
And sneak in startled speed along ;
And beggar, creeping like a snail,
To make his hungry hopes prevail
O'er the warm heart of charity,
Leaves his lame halt and hastens by.

Clare.

CLXXX

THE FROLICSOME OLD DOG

The barking dogs, by lane and wood,
Drive sheep afield from foddering ground ;
And Echo, in her summer mood,
Briskly mocks the cheering sound.

No more behind his master's heels
The dog creeps on his winter-pace ;
But cocks his tail, and o'er the fields
Runs many a wild and random chase,

Following, in spite of chiding calls,
The startled cat with harmless glee,
Scaring her up the weed-green walls,
Or mossy-mottled apple tree.

As crows from morning perches fly,
He barks and follows them in vain ;
Even larks will catch his nimble eye,
And off he starts and barks again,
With breathless haste and blinded guess,
Oft following where the hare hath gone ;
Forgetting, in his joy's excess,
His frolic puppy-days are done !

Clare.

CLXXXI

THE TEASED PET

THE cow-boy still cuts short the day
By mingling mischief with his play;
Oft in the pond, with weeds o'ergrown,
Hurling quick the plashing stone
To cheat his dog, who watching lies,
And instant plunges for the prize;
And though each effort proves in vain,
He shakes his coat, and dives again,
Till, wearied with the fruitless play,
He drops his tail, and sneaks away.

Clare.

CLXXXII

LAMENT OF A POOR BLIND

Hark! hark! the dogs do bark,
The beggars are coming . . . .
OLD BALLAD.

OH what shall I do for a dog?
Of sight I have not a particle,
    Globe, Standard, or *Sun,*
    Times, Chronicle—none
Can give *me* a good leading article.

A Mastiff once led me about,
But people appeared so to fear him—
    I might have got pence
    Without his defence,
But Charity would not come near him.

A Bloodhound was not much amiss,
But instinct at last got the upper;
    And tracking Bill Soames
    And thieves to their homes,
I never could get home to supper.

A Foxhound once served me as guide,
A good one at hill, and at valley;
    But day after day
    He led me astray,
To follow a milk-woman's tally.

A Turnspit once did me good turns
At going and crossing and stopping;
    Till one day his breed
    Went off at full speed
To spit at a great fire in Wapping.

A Pointer once pointed my way,
But did not turn out quite so pleasant,
    Each hour I'd a stop
    At a poulterer's shop
To point at a very high pheasant.

A Pug did not suit me at all ;
The feature unluckily rose up,
    And folks took offence
    When offering pence
Because of his turning his nose up.

A butcher once gave me a dog,
That turn'd out the worst one of any ;
    A Bull-dog's own pup,
    I got a toss up,
Before he had brought me a penny.

My next was a Westminster dog,
From Aistrop the regular cadger ;
    But, sightless, I saw
    He never would draw
A blind man as well as a badger.

A Greyhound I got by a swop,
But, Lord, we soon came to divorces ;
    He treated my strip
    Of cord, like a slip,
And left me to go my own courses.

A Poodle once towed me along,
But always we came to one harbour,
    To keep his curls smart,
    And shave his hind part,
He constantly called on a barber.

My next was a Newfoundland brute,
As big as a calf fit for slaughter;
     But my old cataract
     So truly he backed
I always fell into the water.

I once had a Sheep-dog for guide,
His worth did not value a button;
     I found it no go,
     A Smithfield Ducrow,
To stand on four saddles of mutton.

My next was an Esquimaux dog,
A dog that my bones ache to talk on,
     For picking his ways
     On cold frosty days
He picked out the slides for a walk on.

Bijou was a lady-like dog,
But vexed me at night not a little,
     When tea-time was come
     She would not go home—
Her tail had once trailed a tin kettle.

I once had a sort of a Shock,
And kissed a street post like a brother,
     And lost every tooth
     In learning this truth—
One blind cannot well lead another.

A Terrier was far from a trump,
He had one defect, and a thorough,
    I never could stir,
     'Od rabbit the cur!
Without going into the Borough.

My next was Dalmatian, the dog!
And led me in danger, oh crikey!
    By chasing horse heels,
    Between carriage wheels,
Till I came upon boards that were spiky.

The next that I had was from Cross,
And once was a favourite Spaniel
    With Nero, now dead,
    And so I was led
Right up to his den like a Daniel.

A Mongrel I tried, and he did,
As far as the profit and lossing;
    Except that the kind
    Endangers the blind,
The breed is so fond of a crossing.

A Setter was quite to my taste,
In alleys or streets, broad or narrow,
    Till one day I met
    A very dead set
At a very dead horse in a barrow.

I once had a dog that went mad,
And sorry I was that I got him;
    I came to a run,
    And a man with a gun,
Peppered *me* when he ought to have shot him.

My profits have gone to the dogs,
My trade has been such a deceiver,
    I fear that my aim
    Is a mere losing game—
Unless I can find a Retriever.

Hood.

CLXXXIII

DYING OSCAR

OLD Oscar, how feebly thou crawl'st to the door,
Thou who wert all beauty and vigour of yore;
How slow is thy stagger the sunshine to find,
And thy straw-sprinkled pallet—how crippled
    and blind!
But thy heart is still living—thou hearest my
    voice—
And thy faint-wagging tail says thou yet canst
    rejoice;
Ah! how different art thou from the Oscar of old,
The sleek and the gamesome, the swift and the
    bold!

At sunrise I wakened to hear thy proud bark,
With the coo of the house-dove, the lay of the
     lark;
And out to the green fields 'twas ours to repair,
When sunrise with glory empurpled the air,
And the streamlet flowed down in its gold to the
     sea,
And the night-dew like diamond sparks gleamed
     from the tree,
And the sky o'er the earth in such purity glowed,
As if angels, not men, on its surface abode!

How then thou wouldst gambol, and start from
     my feet,
To scare the wild birds from their sylvan retreat,
Or plunge in the smooth stream, and bring to
     my hand
The twig or the wild-flower I threw from the
     land;
On the moss-sprinkled stone if I sat for a space,
Thou wouldst crouch on the greensward, and
     gaze in my face,
Then in wantonness pluck up the blooms in thy
     teeth,
And toss them above thee, or tread them beneath.

Then I was a schoolboy all thoughtless and free,
And thou wert a whelp full of gambol and
     glee;
Now dim is thine eyeball, and grizzled thy hair,
And I am a man, and of grief have my share!

Thou bring'st to my mind all the pleasures of
    youth,
When hope was the mistress, not handmaid of
    truth,
When earth looked an Eden, when joy's sunny
    hours
Were cloudless, and every path glowing with
    flowers.

Now summer is waning; soon tempest and
    rain
Shall harbinger desolate winter again,
And thou, all unable its grip to withstand,
Shalt die when the snow-mantle garments the
    land :
Then thy grave shall be dug 'neath the old
    cherry-tree,
Which in spring-time will shed down its blossoms
    on thee ;
And, when a few fast-fleeting seasons are o'er,
Thy faith and thy form shall be thought of no
    more !

Then all who caressed thee and loved shall be
    laid,
Life's pilgrimage o'er, in the tomb's dreary
    shade;
Other steps shall be heard on these floors, and
    the past
Be like yesterday's clouds from the memory
    cast.

Improvements will follow; old walls be thrown
    down,
Old landmarks removed, when old masters are
    gone ;
And the gard'ner, when delving, will marvel to
    see
White bones, where once blossomed the old
    cherry-tree !

Moir.

CLXXXIV

THE DOGS' WELCOME

Don and Sancho, Tramp and Tray,
Upon the parlour steps collected,
Wagged all their tails, and seemed to say :
' Our master knows you ; you 're expected ! '

Praed.

CLXXXV

TO FLUSH, MY DOG

Loving friend, the gift of one
Who her own true faith has run,
    Through thy lower nature,
Be my benediction said
With my hand upon thy head,
    Gentle fellow-creature !

Like a lady's ringlets brown,
Flow thy silken ears adown
    Either side demurely
Of thy silver-suited breast,
Shining out from all the rest
    Of thy body purely.

Darkly brown thy body is,
Till the sunshine striking this
    Alchemise its dulness,
When the sleek curls manifold
Flash all over into gold,
    With a burnished fulness.

Underneath my stroking hand,
Startled eyes of hazel bland
    Kindling, growing larger,
Up thou leapest with a spring,
Full of prank and curveting,
    Leaping like a charger.

Leap ! thy broad tail waves a light,
Leap ! thy slender feet are bright,
    Canopied in fringes,
Leap—those tasselled ears of thine
Flicker strangely, fair and fine,
    Down their golden inches.

Yet, my pretty, sportive friend,
Little is 't to such an end
    That I praise thy rareness !

Other dogs may be thy peers
Haply in these drooping ears,
 And this glossy fairness.

But of *thee* it shall be said,
This dog watched beside a bed
 Day and night unweary,—
Watched within a curtained room,
Where no sunbeam brake the gloom
 Round the sick and dreary.

Roses, gathered for a vase,
In that chamber died apace,
 Beam and breeze resigning.
This dog only, waited on,
Knowing that when light is gone
 Love remains for shining.

Other dogs in thymy dew
Tracked the hares and followed through
 Sunny moor or meadow.
This dog only, crept and crept
Next a languid cheek that slept,
 Sharing in the shadow.

Other dogs of loyal cheer
Bounded at the whistle clear,
 Up the woodside hieing.
This dog only, watched in reach
Of a faintly uttered speech,
 Or a louder sighing.

And if one or two quick tears
Dropped upon his glossy ears,
    Or a sigh came double,—
Up he sprang in eager haste,
Fawning, fondling, breathing fast,
    In a tender trouble.

And this dog was satisfied
If a pale, thin hand would glide
    Down his dewlaps sloping,—
Which he pushed his nose within
After,—platforming his chin
    On the palm left open.

This dog, if a friendly voice
Call him now to blither choice
    Than such chamber-keeping,
'Come out!' praying from the door,—
Presseth backward as before,
    Up against me leaping.

Therefore to this dog will I,
Tenderly, not scornfully,
    Render praise and favour:
With my hand upon his head,
Is my benediction said
    Therefore, and for ever.

And because he loves me so,
Better than his kind will do
    Often, man or woman,

Give I back more love again
Than dogs often take of men,
        Leaning from my Human.

Blessings on thee, dog of mine,
Pretty collars make thee fine,
        Sugared milk make fat thee !
Pleasures wag on in thy tail,
Hands of gentle motion fail
        Nevermore, to pat thee !

Downy pillow take thy head,
Silken coverlid bedstead,
        Sunshine help thy sleeping !
No fly's buzzing wake thee up,
No man break thy purple cup,
        Set for drinking deep in.

Whiskered cats arointed flee,
Sturdy stoppers keep from thee
        Cologne distillations ;
Nuts lie in thy path for stones,
And thy feast-day macaroons
        Turn to daily rations !

Mock I thee, in wishing weal ?—
Tears are in my eyes to feel
        Thou art made so straitly,
Blessing needs must straiten too,—
Little canst thou joy or do,
        Thou who lovest *greatly*.

Yet be blessèd to the height
Of all good and all delight
   Pervious to thy nature ;
Only *loved* beyond that line,
With a love that answers thine,
   Loving fellow-creature !

                  E. B. Browning.

CLXXXVI

WELCOMING THE DAWN

     At morning's call
The small-voiced pug-dog welcomes in the sun,
And flea-bit mongrels, wakening one by one,
     Give answer all.

                  Holmes.

CLXXXVII

QUESTIONS

Is there not something in the pleading eye
Of the poor brute that suffers, which arraigns
The law that bids it suffer ?   Has it not
A claim for some remembrance in the book,
That fills its pages with the idle words
Spoken of man ?   Or is it only clay,
Bleeding and aching in the potter's hand,
Yet all his own to treat it as he will,
And when he will to cast it at his feet,
Shattered, dishonoured, lost for evermore ?

My dog loves me, but could he look beyond
His earthly master, would his love extend
To Him who—hush! I will not doubt that He
Is better than our fears, and will not wrong
The least, the meanest of created things.

Holmes.

CLXXXVIII

SCOTT'S DOGS AT MELROSE ABBEY

THERE an old man sat serene,
And well I knew that thoughtful mien
Of him whose early lyre had thrown
Over these mouldering walls the magic of its
    tone.

     *   *   *   *

It was a comfort too to see
   Those dogs that from him ne'er would rove,
And always eyed him rev'rently,
   With glances of depending love.
They know not of that eminence
Which marks him to my reasoning sense;
They know but that he is a man,
And still to them is kind, and glads them all he
    can.

And hence their quiet looks confiding,
   Hence grateful instincts seated deep,
By whose strong bond, were ill betiding,
   They'd risk their own his life to keep.

What joy to watch in lower creature
Such dawning of a moral nature,
And how (the rule all things obey)
They look to a higher mind to be their law
    and stay !

Arthur Hallam.

CLXXXIX

THE WAGGIN' O' OUR DOG'S TAIL

WE hae a dog that wags his tail
  (He's a bit of a wag himsel', O !)
Every day he gangs down the town,
  At nicht he's news to tell, O !
      The waggin' o' our dog's tail, bow-wow!
      The waggin' o' our dog's tail.

He saw the Provost o' the town,
  Parading down the street, O !
Quo' he, 'Ye're no like me, my lord,
  For ye canna see your feet, O !'

He saw a man grown unco poor,
  And looking sad and sick, O !
Quo' he, 'Cheer up, for ilka dog
  Has aye a bane to pick, O !'

He saw a man wi' mony a smile,
  Wi'out a grain o' sowl, O !
Quo' he, 'I've noticed mony a dog
  Could bite and never growl, O !'

He saw a man look gruff and cross,
  Wi'out a grain o' spite, O !
Quo' he, 'He's like a hantle dogs
  Whose bark is waur than their bite, O !'

He saw an M.P. unco proud,
  Because o' power and pay, O !
Quo' he, 'Yer tail is cockit heigh,
  But ilka dog has his day, O !'

He saw some ministers fighting hard,
  And a' frae a bit o' pride, O !
'It's a pity,' quo' he, 'when dogs fa' out
  Aboot their ain fireside, O !'

He saw a man gaun staggerin' hame,
  His face baith black and blue, O !
Quo' he, 'I'm ashamed of the stupid brute,
  For never a dog gets fou', O !'

He saw a man wi' a hairy face,
  Wi' beard and big moustache, O !
Quo' he, 'We baith are towsy dogs,
  But ye hae claes and cash, O !'

He saw a crowd in a bonny park,
  Where dogs were not allowed, O !
Quo' he, 'The rats in kirk and state
  If we were there might rue't, O !'

He saw a man that fleeched a lord,
  And flatterin' lees did tell, O !
Quo' he, 'A dog's owre proud for that,
  He'll only claw himsel', O !'

He saw a doctor drivin' about,
  And ringin' every bell, O!
Quo' he, 'I've been as sick's a dog,
  But I aye could cure mysel', O!'

He heard a lad and leddie braw
  Singin' a grand duet, O!
Quo' he, 'I've heard a cat and dog
  Could yowl as weel as that, O!'

He saw a laddie swaggerin' big,
  Frae tap to tae sae trim, O!
Quo' he, 'It's no' for a dog to laugh
  That ance was a pup like him, O!'

Our doggie he cam' hame at e'en,
  And scarted baith his lugs, O!
Quo' he, 'If folk had only tails
  They'd be maist as gude as dogs, O!'
        The waggin' o' our dog's tail, bow-wow!
        The waggin' o' our dog's tail.

Macleod.

CXC

THE BRAVE DOG'S CHALLENGE

VILE cur, why will you late and soon
    At honest people fly?
You, you, the veriest poltroon
    Whene'er a wolf comes by!

Come on, and if your stomach be
    So ravenous for fight,
I 'm ready !   Try your teeth on me,
    You 'll find that I can bite.

For like Molossian mastiff stout,
    Or dun Laconian hound,
That keeps sure ward, and sharp look-out
    For all the sheepfolds round,

Through drifted snow with ears thrown back
    I 'm ready, night or day,
To follow fearless on the track
    Of every beast of prey.

But you, when you have made the wood
    With bark and bellowing shake,
If any thief shall fling you food
    The filthy bribe you take.

                    Martin (Horace).

CXCI

THE PUPS AND THE FISH

The village dogs and ours, elate and brave,
Lay looking over, barking at the fish ;
Fast, fast the silver creatures took the bait,
And when they heaved and floundered on the rock,
In beauteous misery, a sudden pat
Some shaggy pup would deal, then back away,
At distance eye them with sagacious doubt,
And shrink half-frighted from the slippery things.

                    Jean Ingelow.

CXCII

THE DEAD BOY'S PORTRAIT
AND HIS DOG

DAY after day I have come and sat
Beseechingly upon the mat,
Wistfully wondering what you are at!

Why have they placed you on the wall,
So deathly still, so strangely tall?
You do not turn to me, nor call.

Why do I never hear my name?
Why are you fastened in a frame?
You are the same, and not the same!

Away from me why do you stare
So far out in the distance where
I am not? I am here! Not there!

What has your little Doggie done?
You used to whistle me to run
Beside you, or ahead, for fun!

You used to pat me, and a glow
Of pleasure through my life would go!
How is it that I shiver so?

My tail was once a waving flag
Of welcome! Now I cannot wag
It for the weight I have to drag.

I know not what has come to me.
'Tis only in my sleep I see
Things smiling as they used to be.

I do not dare to bark; I plead
But dumbly, and you never heed;
Nor my protection seem to need.

I watch the door, I watch the gate;
I am watching early, watching late,
Your Doggie still!—I watch and wait!

Massey.

CXCIII

THE PYTHAGOREAN

Going abroad, he saw one day a hound was
    beaten sore;
Whereat his heart grew pitiful: 'Now beat the
    hound no more!
Give o'er thy cruel blows,' he cried; 'a man's
    soul verily
Is lodged in that same crouching beast—I know
    him by the cry.'

Sir Edwin Arnold (Xenophanes).

CXCIV

TO THE TORMENTORS

Dear little friend, who, day by day,
Before the door of home
Art ready waiting till thy master come,
With monitory paw and noise,
Swelling to half-delirious joys,

Whether my path I take
By leafy coverts known to thee before,
Where the gay coney loves to play,
Or the loud pheasant whirls from out the brake
Unharmed by us, save for some frolic chase,
Or innocent panting race ;
Or who, if by the sunny river's side
Haply my steps I turn,
With loud petition constantly dost yearn
To fetch the whirling stake from the warm tide ;
Who, if I chide thee, grovellest in the dust,
And dost forgive me, though I am unjust,
Blessing the hand that smote : who with fond love
Gazest, and fear for me, such as doth move
Those finer souls which know, yet may not see,
And are wrapped round and lost in ecstasy ;—

*   *   *   *

What are ye all, dear creatures, tame or wild ?
What other nature yours than of a child,
Whose dumbness finds a voice mighty to call,
In wordless pity, to the souls of all,
Whose lives I turn to profit, and whose mute
And constant friendship links the man and brute ?
Shall I consent to raise
A torturing hand against your few and evil days ?
Shall I indeed delight
To take you, helpless kinsmen, fast and bound,
And while ye lick my hand
Lay bare your veins and nerves in one red wound,
Divide the sentient brain ;

And while the raw flesh quivers with the pain,
A calm observer stand,
And drop in some keen acid, and watch it bite
The writhing life: wrench the still beating heart,
And with calm voice meanwhile discourse, and
      bland,
To boys who jeer or sicken as they gaze,
Of the great Goddess Science and her gracious
      ways?

Great Heaven! this shall not be, this present hell
And none denounce it; well I know, too well,
That Nature works by ruin and by wrong,
Taking no care for any but the strong,
Taking no care.   But we are more than she;
We touch to higher levels, a higher love
Doth through our being move:
Though we know all our benefits bought by blood,
And that by suffering only reach we good;
Yet not with mocking laughter, nor in play,
Shall we give death, or carve a life away.
And if it be indeed
For some vast gain of knowledge, we might give
These humble lives that live,
And for the race should bid the victim bleed,
Only for some great gain,
Some counterpoise of pain,
And that with solemn soul and grave,
Like his who from the fire 'scapes, or the flood,
Who would save all, ay, with his heart's best blood,
But of his children chooses which to save!

Surely a man should scorn
To owe his weal to others' death and pain?
Sure 'twere no real gain
To batten on lives so weak and so forlorn?
Nor were it right indeed
To do for others what for self were wrong.
'Tis but the same dead creed,
Preaching the naked triumph of the strong;
And for this Goddess Science, hard and stern,
We shall not let her priests torment and burn:
We fought the priests before, and not in vain;
And as we fought before, so will we fight
    again.

Lewis Morris.

CXCV

DISASTERS

'Twas ever thus from childhood's hour!
My fondest hopes would not decay:
I never loved a tree or flower
Which was the first to fade away!
The garden, where I used to delve,
Short-frocked, still yields me pinks in plenty,
The pear-tree that I climbed at twelve
I see still blossoming at twenty.

*   *   *   *

(And then) I bought a dog—a queen!
Ah, Tiny, dear departing pug!
She lives, but she is past sixteen,
And scarce can crawl across the rug.
I loved her beautiful and kind;
Delighted in her pert Bow-wow:
But now she snaps if you don't mind;
'Twere lunacy to love her now.

I used to think, should e'er mishap
Betide my crumple-visaged Ti,
In shape of prowling thief, or trap,
Or coarse bull-terrier—I should die.
But, ah! disasters have their use;
And life might e'en be too sun-shiny:
Nor would I make myself a goose,
If some big dog should swallow Tiny!

Calverley.

CXCVI

WE MEET AT MORN, MY DOG AND I

STILL half in dream, upon the stair I hear
A patter coming nearer and more near,
And then upon my chamber door
A gentle tapping,
For dogs though proud are poor,
And if a tail will do to give command
Why use a hand?

And after that, a cry, half sneeze, half yapping,
And next a scuffle on the passage floor,
And then I know the creature lies to watch
Until the noiseless maid will lift the latch,
And like a spring
That gains its power by being tightly stayed,
The impatient thing
Into the room
Its whole glad heart doth fling,
And ere the gloom
Melts into light and window blinds are rolled,
I hear a bounce upon the bed,
I feel a creeping towards me—a soft head,
And on my face
A tender nose and cold—
That is the way, you know, that dogs embrace—
And on my hand like sun-warmed rose-leaves
    flung,
The least faint flicker of the warmest tongue,
——And so my dog and I have met and sworn
Fresh love and fealty for another morn.

Rawnsley.

A DUMB ADVOCATE

Nature that taught my silly dog, God wat,
Even for my sake to lick where I do love,
Enforced him, whereas my lady sat,
With humble suit before her falling flat,

As in his sort he might her pray and move
To rue upon his lord and not forget
The steadfast faith he beareth her, and love;
Kissing her hand: whom she could not remove
Away that would for frowning nor for threat,
As though he would have said in my behove,
Pity, my lord, your slave that doth remain,
Lest by his death you guiltless slay us twain.

Unknown.

CXCVIII

BOUNCE TO FOP

(FROM A DOG AT TWICKENHAM TO A DOG AT COURT)

To thee, sweet Fop, these lines I send,
Who, though no spaniel, am a friend.
Though once my tail in wanton play,
Now frisking this, and then that, way,
Chanced with a touch of just the tip,
To hurt your lady-lapdog-ship;
Yet thence to think I'd bite your head off,
Sure Bounce is one you never read of.
Fop! you can dance, and make a leg,
Can fetch and carry, cringe and beg;
And (what's the top of all your tricks)
Can stoop to pick up strings and sticks.
We country dogs love nobler sport,
And scorn the pranks of dogs at court.

      *   *   *   *

The worst that envy, or that spite,
E'er said of me is I can bite;
That sturdy vagrants, rogues in rags,
Who poke at me can make no brags;
And that to touze such things as flutter
To honest Bounce is bread and butter.
    While you and every courtly fop
Fawn on the devil for a chop,
I've the humanity to hate
A butcher though he brings me meat.

*   *   *   *

My master wants no key of state,
For Bounce can keep his house and gate.
When all such dogs have had their days
As knavish Pams and fawning Trays.

*   *   *   *

Fair Thames from either echoing shore
Shall hear and dread my manly roar.
    See Bounce, like Berecynthia crowned,
With thundering offspring all around,
Beneath, beside me, and at top,
A hundred sons, and not one Fop!
Before my children set your beef,
Not one true Bounce will be a thief.
Not one without permission feed
(Though some of J——'s hungry breed),
But whatsoe'er the father's race,
From me they suck a little grace:
While your fine whelps learn all to steal,
Bred up by hand on chick and veal.

My eldest-born resides not far,
Where shines great Stafford's glittering star ;
My second (child of fortune !) waits
At Burlington's Palladian gates;
A third majestically stalks
(Happiest of dogs !) in Cobham's walks ;
One ushers friends to Bathurst's door ;
One fawns at Oxford's on the poor.

Nobles, whom arms or arts adorn,
Wait for my infants yet unborn.
None but a peer of wit and grace
Can hope a puppy of my race :
And, oh, would Fate the bliss decree
To mine (a bliss too great for me)
That two my tallest sons might grace
Iülus' side, as erst Evander's,
To keep off flatterers, spies, and panders ;
To let no noble slave come near,
And scare Lord Fannies from his ear :
Then might a royal youth, and true,
Enjoy at least a friend—or two ;
A treasure, which, of royal kind,
Few but himself deserve to find ;
Then Bounce ('tis all that Bounce can rave
Shall wag her tail within the grave.
And though no doctors, Whig or Tory ones,
Except the sect of Pythagoreans,
Have immortality assigned
To any beast but Dryden's hind ;
Yet Master Pope, whom Truth and Sense
Shall call their friend some ages hence,

Though now on loftier themes he sings,
Than to bestow a word on Kings,
Has sworn by Sticks, the Poet's oath,
And dread of dogs and poets both,
Man and his works he 'll soon renounce,
And roar in numbers worthy Bounce.

Unknown.

CXCIX

THE FRIEND OF MAN

WITH eye upraised his master's look to scan,
    The joy, the solace, and the aid of man ;
The rich man's guardian and the poor man's
        friend,
    The only creature faithful to the end.

Unknown.

CC

OLD MOTHER HUBBARD

OLD Mother Hubbard
Went to the cupboard
    To get her poor dog a bone ;
But when she came there
The cupboard was bare,
    And so the poor dog had none.

She went to the baker's
    To buy him some bread,
But when she came back
    The poor dog was dead.

She went to the joiner's
  To buy him a coffin,
But when she came back
  The poor dog was laughing.

She took a clean dish
  To get him some tripe,
But when she came back
  He was smoking his pipe.

She went to the fishmonger's
  To buy him some fish,
And when she came back
  He was licking the dish.

She went to the ale-house
  To get him some beer,
But when she came back
  The dog sat in a chair.

She went to the tavern
  For white wine and red,
But when she came back
  The dog stood on his head.

She went to the hatter's
  To buy him a hat,
But when she came back
  He was feeding the cat.

She went to the barber's
  To buy him a wig,
But when she came back
  He was dancing a jig.

She went to the fruiterer's
  To buy him some fruit,
But when she came back
  He was playing the flute.

She went to the tailor's
  To buy him a coat,
But when she came back
  He was riding a goat.

She went to the cobbler's
  To buy him some shoes,
But when she came back
  He was reading the news.

She went to the sempstress
  To buy him some linen,
But when she came back
  The dog was a-spinning.

She went to the hosier's
  To buy him some hose,
But when she came back
  He was dressed in his clothes.

The dame made a curtsey,
  The dog made a bow ;
The dame said, ' Your servant,'
  The dog said, ' Bow, wow.'

Unknown.

NOTES

NOTES

PART I.—NARRATIVE POEMS

FROM *The Bruce.* Barbour was Archdeacon of Aberdeen in 1375. The text here given is based on the MS. in the Library of St. John's College, Cambridge, the spelling being simplified.

will of wane=*at a loss for shelter*   tyne=*lose*
ger=*cause*   stinting=*delay*

Subjoined is the ending as originally written :—

> Bot the sleuth-hund maid stynting thar,
> And vaueryt lang tyme to and fra,
> That he na certane gat couth ga.
> Till at the last than johne of lorn
> Persauit the hund the sleuth had lorn,
> And said, 'We haf tynt this trauell ;
> To pas forthir may nocht avale.'

John Hardyng also describes how Bruce was hunted with bloodhounds by Edward I.

II

From the *Canterbury Tales*—The Nonnes Preestes.

III

The date of the Manuscript of *Schir William Wallace* in the Advocates' Library at Edinburgh, on which this version is founded, is 1488. Harry was blind, and the MS. is consequently faulty.

Gyllisland=*Gilsland* in Cumberland   wicht=*swift*
sicker=*certain*   yird=*land*
Ledaill=*Leddisdale*   derfly=*vigorously*
hy=*haste*

The original ends thus :—

> The power come, and sodeynly him fand :
> For thair sloith hund the graith gait till him zeid,
> Off othir trade sho tuk as than no heid.
> The sloith stoppyt, at Fawdoun still scho stude ;
> Nor forthir scho wald, fra tyme scho fand the blud.

James I. in 1616 issued an order that no fewer than nine bloodhounds should be kept at Esk for tracking persons.

IV

From Stewart's *Buik of the Cronicles of Scotland*—a metrical version of Hector Boece's History, which was written in Latin and published in Paris in 1526-7. The translation was done by royal command in 1531. The incident described is the theft by the Picts lords of a dog belonging to the Scots King Carthlyntus, who had been having a great hunting-party in the Grampians.

pulchritude = *beauty*   let = *stop*
peir = *equal*, '*fit*'   coronach = *lament*
scorpit = *mocked*   cuir = *care*

For the sake of comparison the last lines are given in the original spelling :—

And thair wes slane, gif I rycht understude
Sextie Scottis that war men of gude ;
Ane hundretht Pechtis fechtand on that plane,
Into that feild that samin da wes slane.

V

Book XIV. of the Odyssey, which describes the visit of Odysseus in disguise to Eumæus, the swineherd.

VI

From *Æsop at Court; or State Fables*, published in 1702. The moral is summed up thus :—

When ministers their prince abuse,
    And on the subjects prey :
With ancient monarchs 'twas in use
    To send them Towser's way.

VII–IX

From the *Fables* known as The Cur, The Horse and the Shepherd's Dog, The Mastiff and the Cook, The Turnspit and the Ox, respectively. As regards VIII., compare Mrs. Peachum to Filch in the *Beggars' Opera* :—' You must go to Hockley-in-the-Hole and Mary'bone, child, to learn valour.' Hockley-in-the-Hole was as famous in Queen Anne's time as Southwark Gardens in Queen Elizabeth's. It was situated in Clerkenwell, on the site of the present Ray-street. The old *Norfolk Drollery* contains some curious lines ' upon a dog called Fuddle, turnspit at the Popinjay in Norwich.' Pitt wrote in his *Art of Preaching* :—

His arguments in silly circles run,
Still round and round, and end where they begun :
So the poor Turnspit, as the wheel goes round,
The more he gains the more he loses ground.

X

This is from a letter which Pope wrote to Henry Cromwell on October 19, 1709, about his dog. ' Histories are more full of examples of the fidelity of dogs than of friends,' he wrote, ' but I will not insist upon many of them, because it is possible some may be almost as fabulous as those of Pylades and Orestes, etc. I will only say that the two most ancient and esteemable books, sacred and profane, extant (viz. the Scripture and Homer) have a particular regard to these animals. That of Toby is the more remarkable, because there was no manner of reason to take notice of the dog besides the great humanity of the author. And Homer's account of Ulysses's dog Argus is the most pathetic imaginable, all the circumstances considered, and an excellent proof of the old bard's good nature. . . . Not unnatural as some critics have said, since I remember the dam of my dog who was 22 years old when she died.' It is interesting to note that Pope's translation of Odyssey was not published until 1725. For the English rendering in this volume of Homer's well-known lines see XXX. Compare also XXIII.

This is included among the narrative poems, for although styled by Goldsmith an Elegy, it does not fulfil the conditions that I have laid down for Part III.

Sir Robert Gunning's daughters were ' the two nymphs' referred to.

Geddes was a Scotch Roman Catholic priest. See the better known English version of the same story, XLV.

From *Posthumous Tales*, XVI.—The Dealer and the Clerk. Compare *The Brough*, XIII. :—

> The dogs, who learn of man to scorn the poor,
> Barked him away from every decent door.

This poem was written in 1786. We are told by Gilbert Burns that ' the tale of the Twa Dogs was composed when the resolution to publish was nearly taken (1786). Robert had had a dog which he called Luath (from Ossian), and was a great favourite. The dog had been killed by the wanton cruelty of some person the night before my father's death. Robert said to me that he should like to confer such immortality as he could bestow upon his old friend Luath, and that he had a great mind to introduce something into the book under the title of "Stanzas to the Memory of a Quadruped Friend." But these plans were given up for the tale as it now stands. Cæsar was merely the creature of the poet's imagination for the purpose of holding chat with his favourite Luath.'

the place, etc. = *Ayrshire*	baws'nt = *white spotted*
thrang = *busy*	gawcie = *thick*
lugs = *ears*	hurdies = *hips*
messin = *mongrel*	snowkit = *searched*
tawted = *shaggy*	moudieworts = *moles*
duddie = *ragged*	howkit = *unearthed*
billie = *boon fellow*	daffin = *folly*
gash = *sagacious*	

Burns makes Luath finely say apropos of the New Year festivities of his master's family :—

> My heart has been sae fain to see them
> That I for joy hae barket wi' them.

In Cervantes' *Exemplary Novels*, first published in 1613, is to be found a dialogue between Scipio and Berganza, 'dogs of the Hospital of the Resurrection in the City of Valladolid, commonly called the dogs of Mahudes.' The two discuss mankind, and when the dawn breaks also resolve 'to meet some ither day.' The conversation of Cervantes' dogs lacks verisimilitude.

XVI

From *Italy*—The great St. Bernard. Mr. Hugh Dalziel has exposed the vulgar error that Barry (the dog referred to) was shot in mistake for a wolf by the 43rd person whose life he saved. As a matter of fact the dog was taken alive in 1815 to Berne, where he was afterwards preserved and placed in the museum. Caroline Fry (see XXV.) has helped to gain immortality for the legend. Compare Longfellow : —

> At break of day, as heavenward,
> The pious monks of Saint Bernard
> Uttered the oft-repeated prayer,
> A voice cried through the startled air,
> Excelsior !

> A traveller, by the faithful hound,
> Half-buried in the snow was found,
> Still grasping in his hand of ice
> That banner with the strange device,
> Excelsior !

XVII

Spencer sent the following lines with his poem (written in 1800) to a lady :—

> Die the dark yew and cypress fair,
>   Which long poor Gelert's ashes shaded,
> And shall the bays I planted there
>   Not sooner far than they be faded?
>
> No dews more soft than morning wears
>   Have dropped, their lowly bloom to cherish ;
> Hallowed by beauty's virgin tears,
>   No bays, not even mine, can perish.

Tradition has it that King John gave Gelert in 1205 to Llewellyn, who was his son-in-law. There is a village called Bedd Gelert near Snowdon, where Gelert's grave is pointed out. For another version of the same story, see XXXII. But the incident described dates from the earliest times, and is commonly considered as merely an Aryan myth. It has come down through various European languages. See XLIII. for a somewhat similar legend, in which instead of a wolf it is an adder that threatens the baby's life. The source of that story is given in the note.

XVIII

Included among the poems of 'Sentiment and Reflection' as an *Incident characteristic of a favourite dog.* Wordsworth's notes :—' This dog I knew well. It belonged to Mrs. Wordsworth's brother, Mr. Thomas Hutchinson, who then lived at Sockburn-on-the-Tees, a beautiful retired situation, where I used to visit him and his sisters before my marriage.' It was written in 1805. See elegy on Music, XCVI. Music, by the by, was the name given by Swift to the Church of England in his *Fable of the Bitches.*

XIX

'The young man,' Wordsworth says, 'whose death gave occasion to this poem, was named Charles Gough, and had come early in the spring to Patterdale for the sake of angling. While attempting to cross over Helvellyn to Grasmere he slipped from a steep part of the rock where the ice was not thawed, and perished. His body was discovered as described in this poem. Walter Scott heard of the accident, and both he and I, without either of us knowing that the other had taken up the subject, each wrote a poem in admiration of the dog's fidelity. His contains a most beautiful stanza :—

> How long didst thou think that his silence was slumber,
> When the wind waved his garment how oft didst thou start!

I will add that the sentiment in the last four lines of the last stanza of my verses was uttered by a shepherd with such exactness, that a traveller, who afterwards reported his account in print, was induced to question the man whether he had read them, which he had not.' Composed in 1805. Miss Cobbe and the Rev. H. D. Rawnsley, Vicar of Crossthwaite, have recently caused a stone to be set up on the spot where Gough's remains were found to commemorate the dog's fidelity, undismayed by the professed discovery that the animal had actually subsisted on the dead body. As a matter of fact, however, dogs have been known to live without taking any nourishment at all quite as long as this one did by his master's side.

XX

See previous note.

XXI

From the *Lay of the Last Minstrel*, Canto III. Earlier in the poem Scott relates that William of Deloraine often—

> By wily turns, by desperate bounds,
> Had baffled Percy's best bloodhounds.

XXII

From *Marmion*. Introduction to Canto IV. Compare—

> The shepherd shifts his mantle's fold
> And wraps him closer from the cold ;
> His dogs no merry circles wheel,
> But, shivering, follow at his heel ;
> A cowering glance they often cast
> As deeper moans the gathering blast.
>
> *Ib.*, Canto I.

XXIII

From *Roderick, the last of the Goths* (compare Landor's Count Julian, Scott's Roderick, etc.), a tragedy founded on Spanish tradition. Roderick, King of the Wisi-Goths, has violated Florinda, the daughter of Count Julian, who calls in the Moors to take vengeance. Roderick escapes from death on the battlefield, and turns monk. The incident here described is his return unrecognised in priestly garb. Rusilla is Roderick's mother, and Siverian his foster-father. Dr. Maginn added a note to his translation of Homer (see XXX.). 'The hound Theron and the man Roderick are far inferior to the hound Argus and the man Ulysses. Argus required no length of time to know his master. Instinct is instantaneous.' On the other hand many who have had experience of dogs would support Southey. In reply to a question as to the probability of such a story as this Byron wrote to Moore : 'As far as I could judge by a cur of my own (always bating Boatswain, the dearest, and, alas ! the maddest of dogs !), I had one (half a *wolf* by the she side) that doted on me at ten years and nearly ate me at twenty. When I thought he was going to enact Argus he bit away the backside of my breeches, and never would consent to any kind of recognition in despite of all kinds of bones which I offered him. So let Southey blush, and Homer too, as far as I can decide upon quadruped memories.' See also X.

XXIV

From *Conte à mon chien*. The authoress is addressing her dog Ranger, who died in 1825 and was duly celebrated in elegiac verse. See CLXXV.

XXV

See note to XVI.

XXVI

From the *Ingoldsby Legends*. William of Orange's life was so saved by his dog, and he ever afterwards kept a spaniel of the same race in his bedroom. In the statues of the Prince a small dog is often to be seen at his feet.—Motley's *Dutch Republic*, Part III., chap vii.

XXVII

From *Darkness*.

XXVIII

From the *Siege of Corinth*.

XXIX

From *Don Juan*, Canto II. Pedrillo was Don Juan's tutor, and he subsequently met the same fate as the spaniel.

XXX

First published in *Fraser's Magazine*, 1838. It is given here instead of Chapman's or Pope's translation as more spirited than the former and more literal than the latter. Maginn republished this and other translations of Homer under the title of ' Homeric Ballads.'

Mr. Ruskin (who, by the by, discourses very pleasantly of the Venetian painters and their dogs in *Modern Painters*, v. part ix. 14-20), has written on the incident : ' The Greeks seem hardly to have done justice to the dog. My pleasure in the entire Odyssey is diminished because Ulysses gives not a word of kindness nor of regret to Argus.' But

> Odysseus saw, and turned aside
> To wipe away the tear ;
> From Eumæus he chose his grief to hide—

as the wanderer did not then wish to disclose his identity. Critics who have opposed the one man authorship theory respecting Homer's work have pointed out that the Odyssey abounds in kindly references to dogs, while the Iliad contains none. Compare X. and XXIII., and see notes.

XXXII

Compare XVII. In Horne's *Orion*, Book I. Canto ii., is the subjoined picturesque description :—

> One day, at noontide, when the chase was done,
> Which with unresting speed since dawn had held
> . . . . . The hound with tongues,
> Crimson, and lolling hot upon the green,
> And outstretched noses, flatly crouched ; their skins,
> Clouded or spotted, like the field bean's flower,
> Or tiger-lily, painted the wide lawn.

XXXIII

From *Arthur*, Book VI. A word of explanation is needed as to this passage, which I have inserted on account of the last two lines, that have become proverbial. Gawaine is the victim of a plot, and is encumbered against his will with the lady as a wife. He is relieved of her by a peasant, with whom she chooses to go, and is subsequently overtaken by the man who demands the lady's hound. Gawaine had previously thrown ' his manchet to a hound with hungry face.'

XXXIV

Ibid., Book III. This is a description of the pursuit of King Arthur by Harold of Mercia.

XXXV

From *Sketches of Natural History*. The poem continues to tell the story of Argus, and concludes :—

> And the dog is still the faithful,
> Still the loving friend of man,
> Ever ready at his bidding,
> Doing for him all he can.

The passage quoted is founded, of course, on the Book of Tobit. See title-page.

XXXVI

'Flush,' says Mrs. Browning, 'was the gift of my dear and admired friend Miss Mitford (see CII., CIII., and CLXXIV.), and belongs to the beautiful race she has rendered celebrated among English and American readers. The Flushes have their laurels as well as the Cæsars—the chief difference (at least the very head and front of it) consisting, perhaps, in the bald head of the latter under the crown.' Flush, who was given to Mrs. Browning shortly before her marriage, 'lies in the vaults under Casa Guidi, dying as he did at Florence of extreme old age.' See CLXXXV.

XXXVII

By permission of Messrs. Macmillan I am able to quote part of *Owd Roä* (Rover), which appeared in the late Laureate's *Demeter* volume, 1889.

mander = *manner*	clemm'd = *clutched*
sneck = *latch*	bublin = *unfledged bird*
lether = *ladder*	

Tennyson's poems abound in references to dogs. One of the best of these is to be found in the *Idylls of the King* (Geraint and Enid) :—

> . . . Growling like a dog, when his good bone
> Seems to be plucked at by the village boys,
> Who love to vex him eating, and he fears
> To lose his bone, and lays his foot upon it,
> Gnawing and growling.

XXXVIII

By permission of Messrs. Smith, Elder & Co. Mrs. Sutherland Orr in her *Handbook to Robert Browning's Works* states that *Tray* describes an instance of animal courage and devotion which a friend of the poet's actually witnessed in Paris. The dog 'is made to illustrate Mr. Browning's ideal of a hero in opposition to certain showy and conventional human types.' In the *Asolando* volume the poet, under the heading *Arcades Ambo*, characterises as a coward the man

> . . . who would have no end of brutes
> Cut up alive to guess what suits
> My case, and saves my toe from shoots.

XXXIX

From Nisami (Alger's *Oriental Poetry*).

XL

By permission of Sir Edwin Arnold. From *Pearls of the Faith*: *Islam's Rosary*. Al-Barr=The Good; one of the 99 beautiful names of Allah.

XLI

By permission of Mr. Robert Buchanan. From *Willie Baird*.

'Do doggies gang to heaven?' Mr. Buchanan reports a conversation he had with George Eliot and George Lewes, apropos of the lady's 'splendid bull-terrier.' George Eliot told an anecdote that the dog's ear was cut by the little son of the animal's old master. The boy was to be punished. 'Wagging his tail,' said the novelist, 'just as he is doing now, for he knows I'm telling about him! the noble fellow rose up, put his paws on the child's shoulders and affectionately licked his face; then looking at his master said plainly in the canine deaf and dumb alphabet, "Don't beat him! please don't! He's only an undeveloped human being; he knows no better, and—I love him!" Could human kindness and magnanimity go further? Yet I don't suppose you will contend that the poor dog's loving instinct was enough to distinguish him from the other "beasts that perish"?

Mr. Buchanan said, 'I'm not sure. Why should not even a dog have a soul like any other respectable Christian?'

'Why not indeed!' exclaimed Lewes; 'I have known many so-called Christians who have neither the amiability nor the discrimination of this dog.'

George Eliot rejoined: 'Then here we halt on the horns of a dilemma. Every one with a large acquaintance with decent and "gentleman-like" dogs (as Launce would put it) must admit their share in the highest humanities; and what is true of them is true, to a greater or less extent, of animals generally. Yet shall we, because we walk on our hind feet, assume to ourselves only the privilege of imperishability? Shall we, who are even as they though we wag our tongues and not our tails, demand a special Providence and a selfish salvation?'—*New York Tribune.*

XLII

By permission of Mr. George R. Sims.

XLIII

This is from the *Story of the Seven Sages*—an Indian Romance, the Sendabad, composed, it is believed, during the Persian dynasty of the Arsacides, which lasted from 256 B.C. to 223 A.D. The Romance is of the nature of the Thousand and One Nights, the stories being told to induce a king to disbelieve the charges made against his son by one of his wives, who resembled Potiphar's wife. It has come down to us in various forms in various European languages. The text here given in modified form is from a MS. in the public library of the University of Cambridge, written about the end of the 14th century, and published by the Percy Society in 1846, Mr. Thomas Wright being the editor. See XVII (and note) and XXXII.

snel=*swift*	solas=*salute*
name=*took*	rygge=*back*
moun=(mowen) *may*	hent=*caught*
yal=*yielded*, i.e. *collapsed*	a-goo=*gone*
wood=*wild*	forlore=*utterly lost*
drowe=*drove*	

An idea of the original spelling may be gained from these lines:—

> Bytwen thaym thare cam a ayer
> A good child and a fayre,
> And zonge hagge hit was,
> A twelmowth holde it was.
> There was no thing syrcurliche
> That the Knyght lovyd so myche.

Adder is written throughout with a prefixed *n*.

Dogs figure in another and earlier mediæval romance—*Sir Tristrem*, by Thomas the Rhymer, of Ercildoune. It is one of the Auchinleck MSS. and was edited by Sir Walter Scott, who gave the approximate dates of the poet's birth and death as between 1226 and 1229 and 1286 and 1299 respectively. The

story of Sir Tristrem must be familiar to all. In this romance
the dog drains the drops of the fatal love potion :—

> An hounde ther was biside
>   That was y-cleped Hodain,
> The coupe he licked that tide,
>   Though doun it sett Brengwain :
> Thai loved al in lide,
>   And ther of were thai fain,
> Togider thai gun abide,
>   In joy and ek in pain
>   For thought :
>   In ivel time to sain,
> The drink was y-wrought.

> Thai loved with al her might,
> And Hodain dede al so.

Brengwain was Ysonde's maid. Later in the poem we read
that King Mark of Cornwall banishes Tristrem, who goes to
Wales and fights for King Triamour and is given a dog.

> The King a welp he brought,
>   Bifor Tristrem the trewe ;
> What colour he was wrought,
>   Now i chill you schewe ;
> Silke nas non so soft,
>   He was red, grene and blewe ;
> Thai that him seighen oft,
>   Of him hadde gamen and glewe,
>   Y wis ;
>   His name was Peticrewe,
> Of him was michel priis.

XLIV

This is based on a manuscript discovered in a collection
formed late in the reign of Henry VI. The Romance contains
1719 lines, and was published by the Percy Society in 1846,
Mr. Halliwell Phillipps being the editor.

wede = *rage*	hent = *caught*
stounde = *sudden*	lorn = *lost*
flemed = *banished*	boot = *booty*
tythand = *happening*	dearworth = *precious*
blin = *cease*	

The ending in the original runs :—

> Syr Rogers corse wyth nobulle delay
> They beryed hyt the tothyr day,
>   Wyth many a bolde barone ;
> Hys hownde wolde not fro hym away,
> But evyr on hys grave he lay,
>   Tylle deth had broght hym downe.

It will be noticed that Sir Roger's Truelove and Greyfriars Bobby each spent seven years on his master's grave. Prof. Blackie's Epitaph on Bobby states that he 'followed the remains of his beloved master to the churchyard in the year 1858, and became a constant visitor to the grave, refusing to be separated from the spot until he died in the year 1872.' (Miss Cobbe's translation).

XLV

Compare XIII. The date of the verses is unknown. Many versions are given. I have followed that favoured by Mr. Halliwell Phillipps.

XLVI

This translation from the *Mahabhârata* (the Indian epic, which consists of 200,000 sixteen syllable lines, and is supposed in part to be as old as Homer) is taken from an anonymous article on 'Indian Epic Poetry,' published in the *Westminster Review* of October 1848. Yudishthira gains the throne of India, but unsatisfied even then sets out for heaven with his five brothers and Draupadi, 'and the seventh was a dog.' All die by the way except the hero and his dog, and they at last arrive at the gate of heaven. Then, to quote Mr. W. R. Alger, we have, 'the culminating point of the poetic literature of the world,' as given in this book. The dog suddenly vanishes, and in his stead stands 'the lord of Death and Justice, Dharma's self.' The hero is thus proved, and all ends well. Sir Edwin Arnold has treated the same theme.

PART II.—SPORTING POEMS

XLVII

From the *Booke of the Dutchesse*.

Foot-hot=*hastily*   forlorn=*recall*

It is sometimes said that Chaucer used the word whelp and dog indiscriminately, and the *Second Nonnes Tale* is quoted in evidence :—

> Thinke on the woman Cananee, that saide,
> That whelpes eten som of the cromes alle
> That from hir Lordes table ben y-falle.

But two different words for dog are used in the original Greek of Matthew xv. 26 and 27, which Wyclif, almost alone among translators, appreciated. Chaucer would have been incorrect had he used the word dog here.

XLVIII

From the *Canterbury Tales*—The Knightes. Alaun is the name of a long extinct species, which, Mr. G. R. Jesse says, were probably brought over by the Northmen and derived originally from the Caucasus, whence it accompanied the fierce fair-haired Alani. *Torettes* or *toretes* from the French touret were the rings on the collars to which the chain was fastened.

XLIX

From the *Boke of St. Albans*, first edition, 1486, by Dame Juliana Berners or Barnes, Prioress of St. Albans, our earliest known poetess. The Dame probably belonged to Sopwell Nunnery, of which the ruins still stand, but little is known of her. It is seldom that the lines are correctly quoted. Subjoined is an exact copy of the original :—

THE PROPERTEIS OF A GOODE GREHOUND.

A grehunde shulde be heded like a Snake
And necked like a Drake
Foted like a Kat
Tayled like a Rat
Syded lyke a Teme
Chyned like a Beme
The first yere he most lerne to fede
The second yere to felde hym lede
The iii yere he is felow lyke
The iiii yere ther is noon sike
The v yere he is good inough
The vi yere he shall holde the plough
The vii yere he will anayle
Grete bikkys for to assayle
The viii yere likladill
The ix yere cart sadyll
And when he is commyn to that yere
Haue hym to the Tanner
For the best hounde that ever bikke hade
At ix yere he is full badde.

I have followed the explanation of Mr. Hugh Dalziel with regard to the 8th and 9th years.

L

These lines are introduced in Stow's *Survey of London* (Strype's edition, 1720) with the following words :—' There were two Bear Gardens, the Old and the New : Places wherein were kept Bears, Bulls, and other Beasts to be baited : As also Mastives, in their several Kennels, are there nourished to bait them. These Bears and other Beasts, are there baited in Plots of Ground scaffolded round for the Beholders to stand safe. For the foulness of these rude Sights, and for that these beastly Combats were usually performed on Sundays, and that so much money was idly thrown away, that might have been better given to the poor, a Poet in the latter time of Henry VIII. made and printed these homely verses, more commendable for his zeal than his poetry.' See note to VIII.

LI

Turberville has translated this from the French of Jaques du Fouilloux, who dedicated his work to Charles IX. It and the following lines are taken from the *Noble Art of Venerie*. Turberville in this book treats, *inter alia*, 'of Blacke hounds aunciently come from Sainct Huberts Abbay in Ardene.' He tells how he 'chanced across a book where there was a blasone which the same hunter gave to his bloodhound called Soygllard'; and he quotes this couplet :—

> My name came first from holy Hubert's race
> Soygllard, my sire, a hound of singular grace.

'The hounds which we call Saint Hubert's hounds are commonly all blacke, yet neuertheless the race is so mingled at these days, that we find them of all colours. These are the hounds which the Abbots of St. Hubert haue always kept some of their race or kind, in honour or remembrance of the saint, which was a hunter with St. Eustace. Whereupon we may conceiue that (by the grace of God) all good huntsmen shall follow them into paradise.'

Compare Scott's *Lady of the Lake*, Canto I. :—

> Two dogs of black St. Hubert's breed
> Unmatched for courage, breath, and speed.

St. Hubert had hunting dogs under his special protection. There were some relics of the Saint at Limé, not far from Soissons, and it was thought that neither man nor beast in the neighbourhood was ever attacked with hydrophobia. It was the custom to go on pilgrimage to the relics each November 2nd, when the following hymn would be sung :—

> Saint Hubert glorieux,
> Dieu me soit amoureux ;
> Trois choses me défend :
> De la nuit du serpent ;
> Mauvais loup, mauvais chien,
> Mauvaises bêtes enragées
> Ne puissent m'approcher,
> Me voir, ne me toucher,
> Non plus qu'étoile au ciel.

Rathe=*soon*   in liam=*in leash*

LIV, LV

Similes from Harington's translation of *Orlando Furioso*. See also CXXVIII. and CXXIX. Compare Elphinston's translation of Martial, Book XIV.

> Like a tumbler that does play
> His game and looks another way.

On the title-page of Harington's folio (1591, First Edition) appears his portrait, and that of a spaniel-like dog with collar and chain. In a note to Book XLI. he acknowledges having taken the idea and the motto *Fin Che Vegna* from the device of Oliver. 'I can alleage,' he says, 'many examples of wise men and some verie great men that have not only taken pictures but built cities in remembrance of serviceable beasts. And as for dogges, Dr. Cavnes (Caius), a learned Phisition and a good man, wrote a treatise of them, and the Scripture itselfe hath voutchsafed to commend Tobias dogge.'

Compare Plutarch's *Life of Themistocles*—the dog's grave.

LVI

From *Poly-olbion*, 23rd song; published in 1619. The scene described is Kelmarsh, in Northamptonshire.

> finder = *hare finder*
> cute = *cur*
> coats = *one hound outstripping another*

In the same poem we have the following lines dealing with Wiltshire-bred dogs :—

> And as the western soil as sound a horse doth breed
> As doth the land that lies betwixt the Trent and Tweed,
> No hunter so but finds the breeding of the west
> The only kind of hounds for mouth and nostril best ;
> That cold doth seldom fret, nor heat doth over-hail,
> As standing in the flight, as pleasant on the trail ;
> Free hunting, eas'ly checked, and loving every chase,
> Straight running, hard and tough, of reasonable pace,
> Not heavy as that hound which Lancashire doth breed,
> Nor as the northern kind so light and hot of speed.

See note to CXXX.

LVII

From the *Midsummer Night's Dream*, Act IV. Sc. I.

> observation = *observance*—of the May-morning rites.
> vaward = *vanward*
> flewed = *possessed of large flews, or chaps*
> sanded = *sandy coloured*
> cry = *pack* (compare *Coriolanus*, Act III. Sc. 3 : You common cry of curs).

LVIII

From the *Taming of the Shrew*, Induction, Sc. 1.
'Trash Merriman' was printed obviously in error in the folio
as 'Brach Merriman.' Mr. Dyce suggested 'trash' (used in
the *Tempest*, Act I. Sc. 2, to mean stop), and this makes good
sense. Brach is nearly always used to denote a bitch. Em-
bossed means wearied.

In the Induction, Scene 2, the lords ask the bewildered
Sly :—

> Or wilt thou hunt?
> Thy hounds shall make the welkin answer them
> And fetch shrill echoes from the hollow earth.
>
> Say thou wilt course; thy greyhounds are as swift
> As breathèd stags, ay, fleeter than the roe.

LIX

From Part II. of *King Henry VI.*, Act V. Sc. 1. Richard
is speaking. There is a double meaning to these words and
the whole passage. In Part III., Act II. Sc. 1, Richard
again takes a simile from bear-baiting.

> As a bear encompassed round with dogs,
> Who having pinched a few and made them cry,
> The rest stand all aloof, and bark at him.

Compare also the *Merry Wives of Windsor*, Act I. Sc. 1.

Slender.—Why do your dogs bark so? Be there bears i' the town?
Anne.—I think there are, sir; I heard them talked of.
Slender.—I love the sport well.

LX

From *Titus Andronicus*, Act II. Sc. 2.

LXI

From *Venus and Adonis*. The goddess has been previously
praying the youth if he needs must hunt to be ruled by her
and 'uncouple at the timorous hare'; upon whose wiles to
deceive 'the hot scent-snuffing hounds' she dwells.

LXII

From the forgotten *Gondibert*, Book I. Canto 2. The
incident described is

> The hunting which did yearly celebrate
> The Lombards' glory and the Vandals' rage,

and took place near Verona.

LXIII

From *Hudibras*, Part I. Canto I.

LXIV

From the *Georgics*, Book III. Compare Dryden's translation of the *Æneid*, Book IV. :—

> They issue early through the city gate,
> Where the more wakeful huntsmen ready wait
> With nets and toils and darts besides the force
> Of Spartan dogs.

In his description of Daphne's flight from Apollo, Dryden likens it to that of a greyhound after a hare :—

> As when th' impatient greyhound, slipt from far,
> Bounds o'er the glebe, to course the fearful hare,
> She in her speed does all her safety lay ;
> And he with double speed pursues the prey,
> O'er-runs her at the fitting turn, and licks
> His chaps in vain, and blows upon the flix.

LXV

From Ovid's *Metamorphoses*, Book VII. Artemis gave Lelaps and a dart to Procris that she might therewith regain the affections of Cephalus, her husband. Another story states that the dog was enrolled among the stars. See note to LXXXVIII.

LXVI

Sir Walter Scott, writing to Thomas Goodlake in 1828, says :—' This elegy turns upon a circumstance which, when I kept greyhounds, I felt a considerable alloy to the sport, I mean the necessity of despatching the instruments and partakers of our amusements when they begin to make up by cunning for the deficiency of youthful vigour.' The poem was printed in James Watson's *Comic and Serious Scots Poems*, Part I., 1706, as 'The last dying words of a famous greyhound in the shire of Fife.' Hamilton of Gilbertfield was the poetical correspondent of Allan Ramsay.

fell=*mettlesome*	pash=*head*
but=*without*	bardy=*contentious*
sery=*eager*	amry sneck=*latch of a pantry*
mackings=*hares*	chafts=*chatterers*
gash=*sagacious*	beddy=*obedient*
felni=*crafty*?	clinck=*seize forcibly*
packy=*familiar*	

LXVII

From Ovid's *Metamorphoses*, Book III. Compare the *Merry Wives of Windsor*, Act II. Sc. 1 :—

> Go thou,
> Like Sir Actæon he, with Ringwood at thy heels.

LXVIII

From a *Fragment of a Poem on Hunting*.

LXIX-LXXI

From the *Fables*, known as The Eagle and the Assembly of Animals, the Hound and the Huntsman, and the Setting Dog and the Partridge, respectively.

The qualities of the spaniel have often been discussed. A writer, unknown to me, has penned the following :—

> How falsely is the spaniel drawn !
> Did man from him first learn to fawn?
> A dog proficient in the trade !
> He, the chief flatterer nature made !
> Go man, the ways of courts discern,
> You 'll find a spaniel still might learn.

On the other hand, in Pope's letter to Cromwell (see Note to X.) occurs this passage :—' Sir William Trumbull has told me a story which he heard from one that was present when our King, Charles I., being with some of his court during his troubles, and a discourse arising what sort of dogs deserved pre-eminence, and it being on all hands agreed to belong either to a spaniel or greyhound, the King gave his opinion on the part of the greyhound, because, said he, it has all the good nature of the other without the fawning.'

LXXIII

I have taken the liberty of transposing one or two of the extracts from Somervile's classic poem, and of inserting cross-heads. 'Somervile,' says Dr. Johnson, 'is allowed by sportsmen to write with great intelligence of the subject which is the first requisite to excellence, and though it is impossible to interest the common readers of verse in the dangers or pleasures of the chase, he has done all that transition and authority could effect.'

PAIRING TIME.—Compare Shakespeare's *Troilus and Cressida*, Act V. Sc. 1 :—'He will spend his mouth, and promise, like Brabler the hound.'

The LITTER.—Compare *Merry Wives of Windsor* (Falstaff): 'The rogues slighted me into the river with as little remorse as they would have drowned a blind bitch's puppies, fifteen i' the litter.'

'With some great title,' compare—

> As mastiff dogs in modern phrase are
> Called Pompey, Scipio, and Cæsar.
>
> *Swift* (A Salamander).

> Our meannesses by lofty names we dignify
> As Jove and Juno may twin puppies signify.
>
> *P. J. Bailey* (The Age).

APOSTROPHE to ARGUS.—See X. and XXX.

HYDROPHOBIA.—Sea-water was long regarded as a remedy for hydrophobia, as was also the application to the wound of a hair of the biter. Compare Gay's *The Mad Dog*.

LXXIV

From *Rural Sports*. Compare *Troilus and Cressida*, Act v. Sc. 7:—

> Now, bull! now, dog! 'Loo, Paris, 'loo!
> The bull has the game: ware horns ho!

Claudian, the last of the Latin classic poets, refers to

> The British hound
> That brings the bull's big forehead to the ground.

Symmachus mentions the presence of British bulldogs at the Coliseum in Rome.

LXXVI

From Martial's *Epigrams*.

LXXVII

Whitaker devotes a chapter in his *History of Manchester* (1771) to dogs, and proves the early excellence of British breeds by quotations from numerous classic authors. Gratius Faliscus was a contemporary of Ovid (B.C. 43—A.D. 18). The extracts here given are translated from the *Cynegeticon Liber*.

Christopher Ware (1645-1711) also translated the work, and in a poetical preface Edmund Waller declared :—

> Here huntsmen with delight may read
> How to chase dogs for scent or speed,
> And how to change and mend the breed.

Whitaker points out that Nemesianus, towards the close of the third century, wrote:—

> Be thine the greyhounds of the British race,
> And taste improved the pleasures of the chase.

LXXVIII

Oppian, the author of the *Cynegetica*, lived *circa* 206. The poem consists of more than 2000 hexameter lines. Authorities are not agreed as to the kind of dog meant by Agasses. One says harriers, another beagles, etc. In the *Living Librarie* of Camerarius, translated by Molle (see CXXIV), it is stated that there was once a ' Procurator or Commissionarie that had charge of the dogs of Britanie in the Emperour's behalfe, and at this day there be some of them found which Camden calleth Agase-hounds, and named Agasæi.' The dogs of Epirus, otherwise Molossian hounds, are frequently mentioned by the ancient writers.

LXXIX

From *Mador of the Moor*, Canto I.—The Hunting. This poem was written to rival Scott's *Lady of the Lake*.

LXXX

From the *Lady of the Lake*, Canto I. See the note to LI.

LXXXI

Ibid., Canto V. See the note to XV.

LXXXII

From Barnes's *Poems in the Dorset Dialect*.

LXXXIII

This fragment is from the oldest known poetical composition in the Manx language.

PART III.—ELEGIAC POEMS

LXXXV

From the *Hesperides*.

LXXXVI

Shock will be recognised as the name of Belinda's dog in the *Rape of the Lock*.

LXXXVII

Blacklock was blind from babyhood.   See CLVII.

LXXXVIII

From Martial's *Epigrams*, Book XI.   Erigone's dog was
called Maera.   Icarius, an Athenian, the father of Erigone,
was taught by Dionysus how to make wine.   The Greek gave
some to the peasants, who became drunk, and, thinking
Icarius had poisoned them, killed him.   They hid the body,
which Erigone afterwards found, conducted to the spot by
Maera.   Lelaps, the Dictian (or Cretan) dog, was given by
Artemis to Procris that she might therewith win back the love
of her husband Cephalus and, according to a legend, was
transformed, as well as Cephalus, into a star.   For a different
version of the story see LXV.   By the 'Dulichian' is meant
Odysseus's Argus (see X. and XXX.).   The Erymanthian boar,
of course, was that destroyed by Heracles.   A more readable
translation by an unknown hand runs as follows :—

> I trained was by masters of the game,
> I' the field no hound more fierce, i' the house more tame ;
> Lydia my name, my owner's right hand held,
> Erigone's dog not me in faith excelled
> Nor Lelaps yet, for whose great truth 'tis told
> By Jove among the stars he was enrolled.
> Like Argus a long life I did not spend
> In sloth, by useless age brought to my end :
> But the fierce tusks of an enragèd boar,
> Like that of Calydon, my entrails tore.
> Nor of my early death do I complain,
> A nobler fate I could no way sustain.

XC

'Fop' belonged to Lady Throckmorton.

XCII

Epitaph on a dog left by a brother officer in the Island of
Minorca on his return to England in 1772.   Erskine was then
a lieutenant in the Royal Navy.

Another distinguished lawyer, Lord Eldon, composed a
Latin epitaph in memory of his dog Cæsar.

XCIII

Burns went in the summer of 1793 on a tour in Galloway
with John Syme.   They stayed at the house of Mr. Gordon of

Kenmore. 'Mrs. Gordon's lap-dog Echo was dead,' Syme wrote. 'She would have an epitaph for him. Several had been made. Burns was asked for one. This was setting Hercules to his distaff. He disliked the subject, but to please the lady he would try.'

XCIV

Lord Grenville wrote these lines in Latin, and a relative of the author is said to have translated them, doubtless under his supervision. I have, therefore, given the epitaph a place here. The 'Belgian race' refers to the Flemish colony that settled in South Wales. Tippoo was a Newfoundland, and the only creature saved from a wreck off Tenby. He swam ashore with his master's pocket-book in his mouth.

XCV

From the *Farmer's Boy*—Autumn. The last line was inscribed on a stone in Euston Park wall.

XCVI

Written in 1805. Wordsworth himself noted: 'The Dog Music died, aged and blind, by falling into a draw-well at Gallow Hill, to the great grief of the family of the Hutchinsons.' See XVIII. for an 'incident characteristic' of Music.

XCVII

Writing from Abbotsford to his son Charles, in October 1824, Scott says:—'Old Maida died quietly in his straw last week, after a good supper, which, considering his weak state, was rather a deliverance. He is buried below his monument, on which the following epitaph is engraved—though it is great audacity to send Teviotdale Latin to Brazen-nose—

> Maidæ marmorea dormis sub imagine Maida
> Ad januam domini sit tibi terra levis.

Scott then appends the translation—' Englished by an eminent hand.' Lockhart states that the monument was a 'leaping-on-stone, to which the skill of Scott's master-mason had given the shape of Maida recumbent. It had stood by the gate of Abbotsford a year or more before the dog died.' The biographer pleads guilty to a share in the authorship of the Latin couplet, the false quantity of which was a nine-days' wonder throughout the country among those concerned in such niceties.

XCVIII

This was written to please Sydney Smith's future wife's mother, Mrs. Pybus, and it is to be feared that this fact influenced the wit, for elsewhere he wrote : ' No, I don't like dogs ; I always expect them to go mad. A lady asked me once for a motto for her dog Spot. I proposed *Out, damnèd Spot*, but, strange to say, she did not think it sentimental enough.' On another occasion, annoyed by the number of dogs in his parish, Sydney Smith inserted in the local paper a fictitious account of a prosecution of a farmer because of his dogs ; and that had the effect of stopping the alleged nuisance.

XCIX

The following from Southey's *Commonplace Book* may be appropriately quoted in this connection : ' What is become of your dog, Sir John ?' said a friend to Sir John Danvers. ' Gone to heaven,' was the answer. ' Then, Sir John, I hope now you will follow him, for he has often followed you.'

C

A translation from the Latin of Vincent Bourne given by Lamb in *A Complaint of the Decay of Beggars in the Metropolis.* Therein Elia writes : ' Those old blind Tobits that used to line the wall of Lincoln's Inn Garden, before modern fastidiousness had expelled them, casting up their ruined orbs to catch a ray of pity, and (if possible) of light, with their faithful dog-guide at their feet,—whither are they fled ? . . . Where hang their useless staves? and who will farm their dogs? Have the overseers of St. L—— caused them to be shot? or were they tied up in sacks, and dropped into the Thames, at the suggestion of B——, the mild rector of ——— ? Well fare the soul of unfastidious Vincent Bourne, most classical, and at the same time most English, of the Latinists !—who has treated of this human and quadrupedal alliance, this dog and man friendship, in the sweetest of his poems, the *Epitaphium in Canem* or *Dog's Epitaph.* Reader, peruse it ; and say if customary sights which could call up such gentle poetry as this were of a nature to do more harm or good to the moral sense of the passengers through the daily thoroughfares of a vast and busy metropolis.'

CII

The authoress of ' Our Village ' sent both this and the following poem to Sir William Elford. She refers to the first verses as ' all that I can recollect of an elegy on the death of my poor dear old Manx shortly after he died, Oct. 1813. God bless him, poor old darling! He was thirteen years of age, and had always lived with me.'

CIII

From the *Ingoldsby Legends*.

CIV

Boatswain died mad. 'So little aware was Lord Byron of the nature of the malady,' says Moore, 'that he more than once with his bare hand wiped away the slaver from the dog's lips during the paroxysms.' The poem was inscribed on the dog's monument in the gardens of Newstead below the following words :—

> Near this spot
> Are deposited the Remains of one
> Who possessed Beauty without Vanity,
> Strength without Insolence,
> Courage without Ferocity,
> And all the Virtues of Man without his Vices.
> This Praise, which would be unmeaning Flattery
> If inscribed over human ashes,
> Is but a just tribute to the memory of
> Boatswain, a Dog,
> Who was born at Newfoundland, May 1803,
> And died at Newstead Abbey, Nov. 18, 1808.

CV

Louis died on September 17, 1854—I believe at Berkeley Castle.

CVI

By permission of Messrs. Macmillan.

CVII

By permission of Messrs. R. Bentley and Son. The dog belonged to the author's son-in-law, the Hon. and Rev. Canon Leigh.

CVIII

By permission of Messrs. Macmillan. Miss Charlotte Williams Wynn, in her *Reminiscences*, records the death of one of her dogs, over whose grave she placed a somewhat different version :—

> Round this sepulchral spot
> Emblems of hope we twine.
> If God be love, what sleeps below was not
> Without a spark divine.

CX

By permission of Messrs. Macmillan. I am precluded from quoting more than a few verses of Mr. Arnold's exquisite poems on dogs. The elegy on the dachshund Geist is perhaps better known than that on Kaiser. In *Poor Matthias* (a canary) allusions are made to Rover, Atossa, and Max—others of the poet's dogs. *Kaiser Dead* first appeared in the *Fortnightly Review* of July 1887. The first verse, of course, alludes to Lord Tennyson and Mr. Lewis Morris. Compare Burns (*Poor Mailie's Elegy*)—

> 'Come, join the melancholious croon
> O' Robin's reed.'

CXI

By permission of Messrs. Kegan Paul, Trench, Trübner, and Co.

CXII

By permission of Mr. George Meredith. This appeared in the volume called *A Reading of Earth*, 1888.

CXIII

By permission of Mr. James Payn. In *Some Literary Recollections*, Mr. Payn remarks of this : 'One of the few poems I ever got paid for was a humorous one which I had the pleasure to see the other day quoted in an American collection of " anonymous and dead authors." It was written upon a great friend of my boyhood, a pointer called " Jock." . . . The proprietor of the object of this eulogy was so pleased with it that he placed it over the dog's tombstone, and much to his annoyance found he had a great deal more to pay the stone-cutter than I had received for the original manuscript.'

CXIV

By permission of the Rev. H. C. Leonard.

CXV

By permission of Mr. W. H. Mallock.

CXVI

By permission of Mr. H. Knight Horsfield. From *In the Gun Room*.

CXVII

These lines appeared in *The Festoon* (1766) under the heading 'Inscription on an urn at Lord Cork's to the memory of the dog Hector.' The inscription is still to be seen in the grounds at Marston, near Frome in Somersetshire, a seat purchased of Sir John Hipperly by the first Earl of Cork. I am indebted to the present Earl for the information that Hector was a greyhound who lived to the age of fourteen years. Lord Orrery, inviting Swift to Marston in 1737, promises the Dean that 'Hector shall fawn on you.' In a letter written in 1733 to Thomas Southerne, his Lordship says: 'My dear old man,— At my arrival at this dear and delightful place (Marston) the great King Nobby brought me home safe . . . and the invincible Hector is faithful and courageous still.' Nobby was a horse whose life was prolonged to the uncommon age of 34, and he also has a monument at Marston.

CXVIII

This famous greyhound, the ancestor of many famous dogs, was pure black. He belonged to Major Topham. Snowball was in his prime in 1799. It is interesting to note that the Major and Lord Orford improved the breed by crossing a greyhound with a bulldog; with the result that at the seventh remove the animal was found to be as fast as ever, but more courageous—'with small ear, whip tail, large and deep chest, and general firmness of muscle' (*H. D. Richardson*). The following lines have been attributed to Scott, but I have been unable to find any evidence of their authorship, or, of course, of the authorship of the epitaph itself :—

> Who knows not Snowball, he whose race renowned
> Is still victorious on each coursing ground?
> Swaffham, Newmarket, and the Roman Camp,
> Have seen them victors o'er each meaner stamp.

Various authors quote from 'an old MS.' this quatrain :—

> The greyhound ! the great hound ! the graceful of limb !
> Rough fellow ! tall fellow ! swift fellow, and slim !
> Let them sound through the earth, let them sail o'er the sea,
> They will light on none other more ancient than thee.

CXIX

A correspondent of *Notes and Queries* mentions that these clever lines were seen by him in MS. about 1814.

CXX

Compare *Much Ado about Nothing*, Act II. Sc. 3 (Benedict, speaking after Balthasar has sung) :—' An he had been a dog that should have howled thus, they would have hanged him.'

PART IV.—MISCELLANEOUS POEMS

CXXI

From the *Canterbury Tales*—The Prologue.   Wastel-bread was bread made of the finest flour.

CXXII

' Maid at command of King James the Fyft be Schir David Lyndesay of the Mont, Knycht, alias Lyoun King of Arms.' George Chalmers argues the date of this poem to be 1536 from the fact that only a bachelor would have allowed Bawtie to lie on his nightgown, or Bagsche to have jumped on his bed ' with claith of gold thocht it was spread.'   The poem was first printed in 1568.   Bagsche was bred by Gordon of Pittarie (Aberdeenshire) and given to the King by his nephew, the fourth Earl of Huntly.

race=*day*	mys=*faults*
Steill=*a servant of the King*	hiest gre=*highest degree*
close=*courtyard*	(comp. *gre*hound)
hog=*sheep in second year*	lave=*rest*
tulzeour=*fighter*	rachis=*hounds that follow*
speir=*inquire*	*by the nose*
perqueir=*perfectly*	steiding=*place*
fang=*bite*	freik=*impertinent fellow*
lautie=*laws*	widdie=*twig halter, i.e.* in
dre=*suffer*	dread I swing on the
gammis=*gums*	gallows
Paice=*Easter*	

The first verse, for example, as originally written runs as follows :—

Allace ! quhome to suld I complayne
  In my extreme necessitie :
Or quhame to sall I mak my maine
  In court, na dog wyll do for me,
  Beseik and sum for cheritie,
To beir my supplicatioune,
  To Scudlar, Luffra and Bawtie,
Now, or the King pas off the town.

CXXIII

'To his loue that controlde his dogge for fawning on hir.'

CXXIV

Translated from the *Living Librarie*, written in Latin by P. Camerarius, Counsellor to the Free State of Nuremberg. The verses end a chapter on 'The industrie and fidelitie of Dogs: their Elogie or memorable praise.' Molle's book was published in 1621, when, according to Thomas Fuller (*Church History*), he was in the inquisition at Rome. Fuller states that Molle went to Rome about 1607, and died there, after being thirty years under restraint, in his 81st year.

CXXV

From the *Epigrams*. 'To my lady Rogerson, on breaking her bitch's leg.'

CXXVI

Ibid. Sir John sent these lines in a letter to Prince Henry in 1608, full of praise of his 'rare dogge Bungey,' that had just died. 'Althoughe,' he says, 'I mean not to disparage the deedes of Alexander's horse I will match my Dogge against him for good carriage ; for if he did not bear a great Prince on his backe, I am bold to saie he did often bear the sweet wordes of a greater Princesse on his necke. . . . Now let Ulysses praise his Dogge Argus, or Tobit be led by that Dogge whose name doth not appear ; yet could I say such things of my Bungey (for so was he styled) as might shame them both, either for good faith, clear wit, or wonderful deedes ; to say no more than I have said of his bearing letters to London and Greenwich, more than an hundred miles. . . . Of all the Dogges near your father's Courte not one hathe more love, more diligence to please, or less paye for pleasinge, than him I write of.' In a postscript he adds : 'I have an excellente picture curiously limned to remaine in my posteritie.' The witty writer is Sir John Davies (see CXXXVI.), who reflects that a would-be poet is less well known than 'Lepidus his printed dog.' Banks's horse was called Moroccus, and was a wonderful beast that could perform all sorts of tricks. There are frequent allusions to him among the Elizabethans. The horse and his master were burnt.

lepus=*hare*   lepos=*joy*

CXXVII

From the *Epigrams*. Compare *Othello*, Act II. Sc. 3:—
'Even so as one would beat his offenceless dog to affright an imperious lion.'

CXXVIII, CXXIX

From *Orlando Furioso* (see LIV. and LV.). A marginal note in Book XLV., v. 121, Third Edition (1634), states that the latter is 'a very apt simile, for a grehound will overcome a mastiue in continuance of fight, as hath been tried.' Grewnd is a common abbreviation of greyhound among old writers.

CXXX

'Cut-tail' was a common name for a dog. Compare Drayton's *The Mooncalf*:—

> They bring
> Mastiffs and mongrels, all that in a string
> Could be got out, or could but lug a hog,
> Ball, Eatall, Cuttail, Blackfoot—bitch and dog,

and the *Shepherd's Sirena*:—'Whistles cut-tail from his play.'

In the latter poem are found these lines:—

> And we have got us dogs
> Best of all the western breed,
> Which though whelps shall lug their hogs,
> Till they make their ears to bleed.

See note to LVI.

CXXXI

From the 10th *Eclogue*.

CXXXII

From *A Midsummer Night's Dream*, Act II. Sc. 1. Compare *Two Gentlemen of Verona*, Act IV. Sc. 1.

> Yet spaniel-like the more she spurns my love
> The more it grows and fawneth on her still.

There is a well-known proverb:—

> A spaniel, a woman, a walnut tree,
> The more you beat them the better they be.

CXXXIII

From *King Lear*, Act III. Sc. 6. See *Ibid.*, Sc. 7 (Cordelia speaking) :—

> My enemy's dog,
> Though he had bit me, should have stood that night
> Against my fire.

CXXXIV

From *Macbeth*, Act III. Sc. 1—Macbeth addressing the murderers. 'Valued file' is equivalent to descriptive catalogue or studbook.

CXXXV

From *Timon of Athens*, Act IV. Sc. 3. Compare *Two Gentlemen of Verona*, Act III. Sc. 1 (Launce) :—'She hath more qualities than a water-spaniel, which is much in a bare Christian.'

CXXXVI

From the *Epigrams.* See note to CXXVI. John Taylor in *The World Runnes on Wheeles* (1630) wrote: 'Many pretty ridiculous aspersions are cast upon dogges, so that it would make a dogge laugh to heare and understand them: as I have heard a man say, I am as hot as a dogge, or, as cold as a dogge; I sweat like a dogge (when, indeed, a dogge never sweats) ; as drunke as a dogge ; hee swore like a dogge; and one told a man once that his wife was not to be beleev'd, for shee would lye like a dogge.'

masty = *mastiff*

CXXXVIII

From *The Shepherd's Pipe*, Eclogue VI. Compare *Much Ado about Nothing*, Act I. Sc. 1 :—'I had rather hear my dog bark at a crow than a man swear he love me.'

CXXXIX

From *Hudibras*, Part II., Canto III.
Agrippa, the author of 'De Occultâ Philosophia,' was born at Cologne. Erastus is said to have had a devil tied to his dog's collar.

CXL

Katherine Philips, known as the matchless Orinda. The Irish wolf-dogs were formerly placed as the supporters of the arms of the ancient monarchs of Ireland. They were collared *or*—with the motto: Gentle when stroked, fierce when provoked (Edward Jesse).

> An eye of sloe, with ear not low,
> With horse's breast, with depth of chest,
> With breadth of loin, and curve in groin,
> And nape set far behind the head—
> Such were the dogs that Fingal bred.

These lines, translated from a Celtic poem which I have not been able to trace, are supposed to describe the long extinct species.

CXLII, CXLIII

From an early edition of Æsop's *Fables* (1666). The fables are given in Latin and French prose, and in Mrs. Behn's verse.

CXLIV

From *Solomon*, Book I.

CXLV

This poem alludes to the plot in favour of the Pretender in 1722. A lame dog was the strongest link in the chain of evidence against Dr. Francis Atterbury, Bishop of Rochester, who in 1823 was deprived of his office and banished. It appeared that some treasonable letters which were intercepted were signed in the names of Jones and Illington, and that a spotted little dog called Harlequin was sent from France (having its leg broken on the journey) to the person who passed under these names. It was proved that the dog in question was for the Bishop. Counsel for Dr. Atterbury argued before the House of Lords that it was well known that the accused 'never loved a dog, nor ever had one'; and that it was absurd to suppose 'that at the time when the Bishop was in affliction for the death of his wife (the lady had just died) he should indecently discover so much grief for such a trifle'—one of the incriminating letters referring to the writer's tribulation at the sufferings of Harlequin. All the circumstances are fully reported in Howell's *State Trials*, vol. XVI. This was Swift's first contribution to party warfare for nine years. He mercilessly ridiculed the proceedings on the Bill of Attainder in Gulliver's Voyage to Laputa, Chap. VI.; in the Academy of Lagado a lame dog signifies an invader.

Plunkett and Skean or Skinner were two of the chief witnesses before the Privy Council; Neynoe, a third, was drowned attempting to escape.

The proverbial references to dogs will be readily recognised. Compare, for instance, *Hamlet*, Act v. Sc. 1.

> Let Hercules himself do what he may,
> The cat will mew, the dog will have his day;

and Kingsley's *Invitation* :—

> Helping, when you meet them,
> Lame dogs over stiles.

This was not the first time that bishops had been likened to dogs. Howell, the Historiographer-Royal to Charles II., wrote to Lord Clifford from Edinburgh in 1639 : 'The bishops are gone to wrack, and they have had but a sorry funeral. The very name is grown so contemptible that a black dog if he hath any white marks about him is called *Bishop*.'

CXLVI

This poem was written in ridicule of Ambrose Philips' poem on the Hon. Miss Carteret, with the object, so it was said, 'of affronting the lady of Archbishop Boulter.'

CXLVII

From the *South Sea Project*.

CXLVIII

Tiger was Mrs. Dingley's favourite lap-dog. He appears in the lines written to celebrate '*Bec's Birthday*' (Nov. 8, 1726) :—

> But when her breakfast gives her courage,
> Then think on Stella's chicken porridge—
> I mean when Tiger has been served—
> Or else poor Stella may be starved.
>
> May Bec have many an evening nap
> With Tiger slobbering in her lap;
> .   .   .   .   .
> Still be she curious, never hearken
> To any speech but Tiger's barking.

Bec (Mrs. Dingley) was Stella's friend and companion.

CXLIX

From *The Gentle Shepherd*.

CL

Miss Cobbe quotes the following epitaph on Robert Mossen-
dew, gamekeeper, inscribed on a mural tablet in Harefield
Church, Middlesex, dated 1744. The last four lines are evid-
ently copied from Gay :—

> In frost, and snow, through hail and rain,
> He scoured the woods, and trudged the plain ;
> The steady pointer leads the way,
> Stands at the scent, then springs the prey ;
> The timorous birds from stubble rise,
> With pinions stretched divide the skies :
> The scattered lead pursues the sight,
> And death in thunder stops their flight.
> His spaniel, of true English kind,
> With gratitude inflames the mind ;
> This servant in an honest way,
> In all his actions copied Tray.

CLI

Pope wrote from Bath in 1736 to George Lyttelton threaten-
ing to ' come to you in the most outrageous spirits and overturn
you like Bounce when you let her loose after a regimen of
physic and confinement. I am very glad that his Royal
Highness (Frederick, Prince of Wales) has received two such
honourable presents at a time as a whelp of hers and the
freedom of the city.' See CXCVII. and note.

CLII

From *An Essay on Man*, Epistle I. Comp. *Ibid.*, Epistle
IV. :—

> Go, like the Indian, in another life
> Expect thy dog, thy bottle and thy wife.

CLIII

The beginning of a poem entitled *The Officious Messenger.*

CLV

From *Tom Thumb the Great*, Act I. Sc. 6.

CLVI

From *Variety : A Tale for Married People.* Telemachus
was the son of Ulysses.

CLVIII, CLIX

From Martial's *Epigrams*, Books XIV. and I. respectively. *Issa* is not exactly one of Elphinston's masterpieces. A better rendering, though anonymous, is that given in Bohn's translation, which begins :—

> Issa's more full of sport and wanton play
>   Than the pet sparrow by Catullus sung ;
> Issa's more pure and cleanly in her way
>   Than kisses from the amorous turtle's tongue.

Pub is the poet's playful abbreviation of Publius.

CLX

From the *English Bulldog, Dutch Mastiff and Quail.*

CLXI, CLXII

Beau died of old age at the end of 1796, and was stuffed. Hayley expressed a hope that the animal thus preserved might ' make a pleasing and salutary impression on the poet's reviving fancy.' See XII.

CLXIII

From *The Task*—The Winter Morning's Walk.

CLXIV

' The dog is my delight (wrote Wolcot) ; you tread on his tail or foot, he expresses, for a moment, the uneasiness of his feelings, but in a moment the complaint is ended. He runs around you ; jumps up against you ; seems to declare his sorrow for complaining, as it was not intentionally done ; nay, to make himself the aggressor ; and begs, by whinings and lickings, that master will think of it no more. Many a time, when Ranger, wishing for a little sport, has run to the gun, smelt it, then wriggling his tail, and, with eyes full of the most expressive fire, leaped up against me, whining and begging, have I, against my inclination, indulged him with a scamper through the woods or in the field ; for many a time he has left a warm nest, among the snows of winter, to start pleasure for me. Thus is there a moral obligation between a man and a dog.'

CLXVI

From *The Lower World.*

CLXVII

From *Auguries of Innocence*.

CLXVIII

From the *Villagers' Verse Book*, originally written for Sunday-school children to learn.

CLXIX

From *The Farmer's Boy*—Winter.

CLXX

From *Marmion*, Canto III.—dedication to James Skene, of Rubislaw. Miss Cobbe states that the son of Mr. Skene has in his possession pictures of both these dogs.

CLXXI

For long prose article on Hector, his father Sirrah, and his son Lion see the Ettrick Shepherd's *Calendar*. Hogg says Hector was rather of a small size, very rough and shagged, and not far from the colour of a fox.

dung = *dejected*	snoovin' = *with bent head*
thraward = *perverse*	heezle-rung = *hazel-stick*
thrawn = *ill-tempered*	thole = *bear*
flare = *cajolery*	biel' = *shelter*
skaithly = *hurtful*	gousty = *boastful*

CLXXII

Landor, who was very fond of dogs, favoured particularly Pomeranians.

CLXXIII

From *Poor Andrew*. Compare Hood's poem *The Bachelor's Dream*, addressed to Puss and Tray. The first verse runs :—

> My pipe is lit, my grog is mixed,
> My curtains drawn, and all is snug ;
> Old Puss is in her elbow-chair,
> And Tray is sitting on the rug.
> Last night I had a curious dream—
> Miss Susan Bates was Mistress Mogg ;
> What d' ye think of that, my Cat ?
> What d' ye think of that, my Dog ?

CLXXIV

Sent to Sir William Elford in 1816.

CLXXVI

From *To Ranger*.

CLXXVII

From *Don Juan*, Canto I.

CLXXVIII

Set to music by the Chevalier Neukomm.

CLXXIX–CLXXXI

From the *Shepherd's Calendar*. The first suggests a passage in *Lear*, Act IV. Sc. 6.

> *Lear.*—Thou hast seen a farmer's dog bark at a beggar?
> *Gloucester.*—Ay, sir.
> *Lear.*—And the creature ran from the cur. There thou mightst behold the great image of authority. A dog's obeyed in office.

CLXXXII

Nero was a lion at the Zoological Gardens. Near Ramsgate Hood and a friend passed a board on which was painted in large letters BEWARE THE DOG. The dog was not to be seen, so Hood picked up a piece of chalk and wrote WARE BE THE DOG? Lamb took charge of Thomas Hood's dog Dash, and the animal fairly tyrannised over the gentle Elia until Mr. Coventry Patmore's father came to the rescue at the entreaty of Miss Lamb, who said: 'If we keep him much longer he'll be the death of Charles.'

CLXXXIV

From *Our Vicar.*

CLXXXV

See note to XXXVI.

CLXXXVI, CLXXXVII

By permission of Dr. O. W. Holmes. The first is from *The Troubles of a Sensitive Man.*

CLXXXVIII

Arthur Hallam visited Scott in August 1829, and wrote the stanzas in memory of a visit to Melrose Abbey with Sir Walter.

CLXXXIX

This poem, in which (says the author's brother, Dr. Donald Macleod) were embodied the supposed reflections of his dog Syke upon men and manners, was frequently sung by Dr. Norman Macleod in the later years of his life. The earnest, meditative countenance, and the quaint accentuation with which he rendered it, accompanied by a suggestive twirl of his thumb to indicate the approving wag of the tail, lent indescribable drollery to the words. The air was ' The barrin' o' the door.'

hantle=*many*   fleeched=*flattered*

CXC

By permission of Sir Theodore Martin. A translation of Epode VI.: to Cassius Severus. Laconian and Spartan hounds are, of course, the same. See note to LXXVIII.

CXCI

From *Brothers and a Sermon.* The fish alluded to are ' syle,' or young herring.

CXCII

By permission of Mr. Gerald Massey.

CXCIII

By permission of Sir Edwin Arnold. From *Poets of Greece.* The original was written by Xenophanes, who lived about 540 to 500 B.C.

CXCIV

By permission of Mr. Lewis Morris, from *Songs of Two Worlds*, 3rd series, 1875. Mr. Morris has written another poem against vivisection, and has called it ' In a Laboratory.'

CXCV

By permission of Mrs. C. S. Calverley. This poem appeared in *Verses and Fly Leaves*, 1887.

CXCVI

By permission of the Rev. H. D. Rawnsley.

CXCVII

The approximate date of this is 1530-1550. It appeared in the first poetical miscellany published in the English language, and was entitled: 'The Louer praieth pity, showing that nature hath taught his dog as it were to sue for the same by kissing his ladies handes.'

CXCVIII

Although this poem is probably by Pope, there can be no certainty in the matter, so I have described it as unknown. It is not included in Mr. Courthope's standard edition of Pope; but, on the other hand, Mr. John Underhill has excluded it from his new edition of Gay (among whose works it is generally found) justifying the omission on internal evidence. Evander is represented in the Æneid, Book VIII., as accompanied by two guardian-dogs. Dryden's hind is, of course, an allusion to 'The Hind and the Panther'—'A milk-white hind, immortal and unchanged.' 'Sticks' in later reprints of the poem is spelt Styx. Spence says Bounce was a great Danish dog. He records Mrs. Racket's statement: 'When my brother's faithful dog and companion in these walks died, he had some thoughts of burying him in his garden, and putting a piece of marble over his grave, with the epitaph

O Rare Bounce!

and he would have done it, I believe, had not he apprehended that some people might take it to have been meant as a ridicule of Ben Jonson.' Blaze relates that Pope discovered his servant in the act of burglary, thanks to Bounce. Pope wrote to Lord Orrery from Twickenham in 1744: 'I dread to inquire into the particulars of the fate of Bounce. Perhaps you concealed them, as heaven often does unhappy events, in pity to the survivors, or not to hasten my end by sorrow. I doubt not how much Bounce was lamented. They might say, as the Athenians did to Arcite in Chaucer :—

Ah Arcite! gentle knight, why wouldst thou die,
When thou hadst gold enough, and Emily?

Ah Bounce! ah gentle beast, why wouldst thou die,
When thou hadst meat enough, and Orrery?

for what in nature could Bounce want at Marston?' Lord Orrery was 'a peer of wit and grace,' else he could not have had a puppy of the race of Pope's Bounce. See CLI.

Bounce was the name of another well-known dog—that of Collingwood, who after his elevation to the peerage wrote : I am out of all patience with Bounce. The consequential airs he gives himself since he became a right hon. dog are insufferable. He considers it beneath his dignity to play with commoners' dogs, and truly thinks that he does them grace when he condescends to lift his leg against them. This I think is carrying the insolence of rank to the extreme, but he is a dog that does it.' Bounce was in action on the *Royal Sovereign* in 1805.

CXCIX

Mr. G. R. Jesse states that these lines have been attributed to Crabbe.

CC

I have followed the text of Mr. Halliwell Phillipps. The date of the poem is unknown. An edition dated 1793 was found among the late Mr. G. A. H. Dean's papers after his death. Messrs. Dean and Son inform me that none like it has been discovered. An anthology of poems about dogs would hardly be complete without Mother Hubbard ; and that is my apology for including it.

INDEX OF AUTHORS

INDEX OF FIRST LINES

INDEX OF DOGS

MENTIONED BY NAME IN THE POEMS

SPECIES OF DOGS MENTIONED*

* Not necessarily distinct.

First Chronicle Books LLC edition, published in 2005
Originally published in 1893 by David Nutt
All rights reserved. No part of this book may be reproduced in any
form without written permission from the publisher.

Library of Congress Cataloging-in-Publication Data available.
ISBN 0-8118-4246-0

Manufactured in China
Jacket design by Benjamin Shaykin

Distributed in Canada by Raincoast Books
9050 Shaughnessy Street
Vancouver, British Columbia V6P 6E5

10 9 8 7 6 5 4 3 2 1

Chronicle Books LLC
85 Second Street
San Francisco, California 94105
www.chroniclebooks.com